# What People Are Saying About This Book

"Carol Chapman and Suzanne Tulien have done the seemingly impossible. They've created a powerful opportunity for readers to completely transform their businesses from the inside out. Brand DNA is a step-by-step guide to creating a bulletproof brand. It uses story, exercises, and direct consulting wisdom to explore the foundations and daily care needed to take your company well beyond the next level.

I write about great national and international brands like Starbucks and The Ritz-Carlton Hotel Company. Brand DNA is the blue print to propel your business to that level of brand preeminence. This book will be a valued resource for me for years to come."

> —Dr. Joseph Michelli, customer experience expert and best-selling author of books like *The New Gold Standard* and *The Starbucks Experience*

"Brand DNA guides the reader in not only defining their unique brand but living their brand in every aspect of their business; an often overlooked key component in building long-term success."

> —T. Harv Eker, Author of #1 NY Times Bestseller *Secrets of the Millionaire Mind*

"Finally, a book that provides exceptional brand 'conversation' in an easy to understand guide with practical exercises for business owners and their employee teams to create genuine brands that are based on real substance and not marketing hype."

> —Duane E. Knapp, Chairman of BrandStrategy, Inc. and the author of *The BrandMindset®* and *The BrandPromise®* books

"If you read a dozen or so books on branding, you'll pick up a lot of the ideas presented in this book. HOWEVER, what you won't get is seeing all those ideas applied to a single case study. Meg's world is a small body care business started by a budding entrepreneur who gets it that the sooner she grasps how branding impacts her business the better off her business will be. She goes through the ups and downs of creating a solid "brand DNA," so as she says, she has a stake in the ground to shape all the strategic decisions she needs to make about her business. It's a great read, and you find yourself cheering Meg on as she moves through the process, all the while, understanding why brand development is a short cut to any small enterprise's business success."

—Janelle Barlow, Best-selling Author, *Branded Customer Service*, 2004 and *A Complaint Is a Gift*, 2008

"I guarantee, in your hands is a book that will take you on a deep dive to discover what you stand for as a brand. Carol and Suzanne's practical 'Brand DNA' step-by-step process will result in serious aha's, enabling you to create a competitive difference in the way your business delivers to your customers and employees. I know first-hand, as Brand Ascension has been our partner in building our brand for more than four years and we're experiencing great results."

—Jim Heneghan, SVP Advertising Sales, Charter Media, Division of Charter Communications

"If you think you knew branding forget it! Once you read this book you will understand in order to survive and thrive, you need to create a paradigm shift in your thinking on what a brand really is. This book will totally change the way you go about defining and building a highly successful and sustainable brand from the inside out!"

—John Baily, CEO Global Underground

"Marketing is only one facet of building Charter Media's success, the other is ensuring we live and breathe the brand we claim to be. In Brand DNA, this critical concept is illustrated clearly and guides the reader in not only defining their unique brand but living it in every aspect of their business; every business can leverage what this process has to offer."
—Patty Bullington, Director Corporate Marketing for Charter Media, Division of Charter Communications

"Brand DNA is a cutting-edge concept and process that will help every business leverage their unique brand attributes to create consistent, relevant and distinctive experiences that will keep your customers coming back for more. At Furry Friends *we* increased our daily deliveries 500% since we went through the Brand DNA program. Every day we get more customer referrals and our business continues to grow."
—Debbie Brookham, Owner, Furry Friends, Inc.

"So many businesses make promises that they can't deliver on. Carol and Suzanne's Brand DNA book and process is a practical and thought-provoking guide to build your business brand from the inside out, so you can deliver on your promises without fail. We're an online business. I can't say enough about their Brand DNA methodology and how it has helped us create more consistency and distinctiveness in how we deliver to our customers at every touch point."
—Cyndi Stout, Owner, Promoz.com

"Having been in business for fourteen years and being lucky enough to achieve moderate success, caused me to get complacent to new ideas and directions for our company. In meeting with Carol and Suzanne, they were able to open my eyes and showed me that my success had caused me to literally sleep walk through new opportunities and possibilities that were out there waiting for my discovery. Carol and Suzanne's Brand DNA process revolutionized me and my team to the point that we will never do business the same again! It opened the door to a world of awareness that changed the way we show up to our customers, vendors and employees from the smallest of details to the largest of campaigns. This book will enable you to see your brand (your world) in a whole new way. It will give you the tools to think, act and show up like an authentic brand to build customer loyalty and employee excitement forever!"

    —Bart Hanks, CEO of Solar Wavz

"Brand DNA is an easy to implement approach to define and build a consistent and distinctive brand in any economy and industry. Trust me—I've been through the process with my team and experienced some big "aha's". You'll find surprising insights, step-by-step exercises and tools that are invaluable to grow and sustain your brand for real competitive advantage."

    —Barbara Harris, Owner, Barbara Harris Team, Harris Group
    Realty, Inc.

"This is a must read book for any entrepreneur! With a business as unique and controversial as Quick Gym, it has proven to be a huge challenge to define our niche in the fitness industry. Working with Suzanne and Carol has proven to be extremely vital in differentiating between marketing and branding, and why we need to know. It has changed our perspective on how to grow our business. Carol and Suzanne's brand DNA process helped us obtain real success through several key learning points, especially by defining exactly who we are, thus optimizing the entire experience we deliver to our customers."

    —Kaja & David Lee Coleman, Owners, Quick Gym Colorado
    Springs

"Building a brand is more than getting a logo, building a website and creating an advertising message. Building a brand is about digging deep beneath the surface to discover your brand's unique attributes: your values, style, standards and differentiators; then leveraging them through a compelling brand platform and promise. Brand DNA delivers a compelling message and provides the tools to help small business owners and their teams build a strong brand that they can readily embrace and consistently deliver on.

—Jane Peck, RN, MBA,Practice Administrator, Endodontic Specialists, Affiliate Faculty, Regis University, College for Professional Studies, School of Management, MBA – Heath Care Management

"From the very beginning when I started Yacht Charter Advisor Carol and Suzanne and their Brand DNA methodology was there to profoundly guide the company spirit and behavior; it's essence. Defining the unique Brand DNA for our online business has provided excellent context to conversations, images, articles and all sensory types…and business decisions. Since going through the brand DNA methodology, it has helped us create a distinctive experience when Charter Pros do business with us. The Brand DNA methodology and book is essential for every small business wishing to enhance their bottom line."

—Stephen R. Austin, Principal & Founder, Yacht Charter Advisor

"As a trademark attorney, I find many clients think selecting and registering a trademark for their product or service is creating a brand. While a trademark is a brand ambassador, it is just one component of a brand. Brand DNA will help you get clear on your brand message and how to deliver on it day in and day out-consistently."

—Brenda Speer, Attorney at Law, Brenda L. Speer, LLC

# BRAND DNA

# BRAND DNA

Uncover Your Organization's Genetic
Code for Competitive Advantage

CAROL CHAPMAN AND SUZANNE TULIEN

iUniverse, Inc.
New York   Bloomington

**Brand DNA**
**Uncover Your Organization's Genetic Code for Competitive Advantage**

*Publisher's Cataloging In Publication*
*Chapman, Carol E. and Tulien, Suzanne M.*
*(cataloging info below)*

*Cover Design: Suzanne Tulien, the Brand Ascension Group*
*iUniverse books may be ordered through booksellers or by contacting:*

*iUniverse*
*1663 Liberty Drive*
*Bloomington, IN 47403*
*www.iuniverse.com*
*1-800-Authors (1-800-288-4677)*

*Because of the dynamic nature of the Internet, any Web addresses or links contained in this book may have changed since publication and may no longer be valid. The views expressed in this work are solely those of the author and do not necessarily reflect the views of the publisher, and the publisher hereby disclaims any responsibility for them.*

*ISBN: 978-1-4502-2063-7 (pbk)*
*ISBN: 978-1-4502-2065-1 (cloth)*
*ISBN: 978-1-4502-2064-4 (ebook)*

*Library of Congress Control Number: 2010905426*

*ATTN: Quantity discounts are available to your company, educational institution, or association, for reselling, educational purposes, subscription incentives, gifts, or fundraising campaigns. For more information please contact: The Brand Ascension Group, LLC at info@BrandAscension.com.*

*Printed in the United States of America*

For every brave, motivated, and inspired entrepreneur
who desires to define, create, and build the best brand experiences
in their industry and is dedicated to walk their brand talk.

And,

To Michael and Jon;
we are forever grateful for your enduring support!

# Contents

# FOREWORD

As the Director of the Colorado Springs Small Business Development Center, I've had the opportunity to meet with hundreds upon hundreds of entrepreneurs and help them through the various stages of business; everything from desire to departure.

I love working with entrepreneurs because more often than not they have a gleam of excitement in their eye, and a hope that tomorrow will somehow be better than today, regardless if today was the worst day of their life or the best day they've ever had. Often, fueled by their passion and sheer will, and as energetic as someone who has consumed three cans of Red Bull®, entrepreneurs drive our economy, change the way we live, and inspire those around them to greatness. However, that being said, highly successful entrepreneurs are laser- focused, channeled away from the 'shiny objects' and zero in on the realities of running a real business.

While in college, I remember getting on a big weightlifting kick and wanting to be huge and muscular like the monstrous body builders on the cover of *Muscle Magazine*. While working out in the gym, I noticed a 'muscle head' on the bench press across the room lifting more weight than I could ever dream of. With my eyes wide and mind envious of his enormous, chiseled chest, I couldn't help but wonder how he achieved that level of muscular definition. I thought he was who I wanted to be.

This 'gym rat' fit right into the stereotype with all the trendy weightlifting attire of the mid 90s—you know, the extra wide weight belt, the cool cross trainer shoes and the stylish, baggy workout pants that were all the rage. His shirt, a sleeveless tank top, was so loose fitting it revealed all the definition in his chest, back, shoulders and arms. He was the closest thing this small Midwest gym had seen to one of those idolized muscled figures we'd seen in movies on the California beaches or on that trendy Muscle Magazine cover. I was awestruck.

I left there thinking to myself, if I want to be huge and have a ripped chest like that guy I have to change the way I look. I'd start with getting some cool workout pants and finding a shirt like his. I assumed that if I came back dressed like him, everyone in the gym would gawk in admiration of me, just as I had of him, while I benched an enormous, well maybe somewhat impressive, okay, it would be a measly 135 pounds. But, I'd still be noticed because of how I dressed.

Looking in a mirror, it was then when I realized changing my dress wouldn't make me like that 'muscle head' I admired. My genetics were different. No amount of weight lifted, protein shakes consumed, or vitamins swallowed would ever result in developing the massive chest my new idol had. It just wasn't who I truly was, according to my DNA. I'd be forcing something I thought others wanted to see from me.

So, what's my point? Many of the businesses I counsel suffer from the same problem I had back then in the gym. They believe that if they dress up their business through a clever marketing campaign, with the cool click pens displaying their logo, or even a flashy website, slick full color brochure or full page ad, their customers would perceive their business as 'the' place to go.

The truth of the matter is, we've all seen businesses pretending to be something they aren't.

Companies that spend thousands of dollars advertising "great customer service" or other expectations, yet provide a mediocre or even horrible experience burn customer trust. They then wonder why their customers aren't returning, and then proceed to spend more money on advertising. Companies like these have on all the right attire, but have no real 'muscle under the shirt.' Our customers want something real, an experience that is genuine and honest. They want and expect consistency in what they actually experience compared to what is promised in the marketing message.

Hence, Brand DNA is a must read for every entrepreneur. As I personally experienced along with my SBDC employee team, Carol and Suzanne give you a step by step process to uncover your organization's genetic code, so you can build and develop the internal muscles needed to fill out and live up to the 'clothes' or 'trade dress' you want your organization to wear.

Though the principles in *Brand DNA* will span the test of time, they are as timely as ever. Demanded by a changing economy, a much more global reach, and an increasing level of discerning customers with numerous choices, stabilizing the message you present and keeping it consistent with your organization's DNA is a key component many businesses are missing toay.

Customers want to do business with brands they trust. That trust is built on being consistent with what you say you are through your behaviors, leadership, systems and employee culture. After immersing yourself into discovering and defining your brand's DNA, you will have your organization's unique genetic code to design the look and feel of a true, authentic, yet differentiated business and literally walk your brand talk!

**Matthew Barrett**
**Director, Small Business Development Center**
**Colorado Springs, Colorado**

# ACKNOWLEDGEMENTS

We want to thank all of the thought leaders before us who have written books and articles and conducted research on the topic of branding. To name a few, Janelle Barlow and Paul Stewart, *Branded Customer Service*, Duane Knapp—*The BrandMindset® and The Brand Promise®*, Martin Lindstrom, *Brand Sense*, Joseph Pine II and James H. Gilmore, *The Experience Economy*, Al Ries & Laura Ries, The *22 Immutable Laws of Branding*, Brad Van Auken, *Brand Aid*. We have learned a lot through their work and research. We have also learned much through our own research and experiences on the leading practices of successful power brands.

This plethora of research and experiences led us to the creation of a proven, flagship internal brand-building methodology—Brand DNA (Dimensional Nucleic Assets®), which we have used successfully with our clients to help them build their authentic brands. As a result, we appreciate all that we have learned and applied to help our clients build an authentic brand—one that is true to what they stand for and delivers consistently on what they promise their employees and customers.

One of our primary beliefs about successful branding is that it starts from the inside out, first defining with crystal clarity what the brand stands for—a unique Brand DNA of style, values, differentiators, and standards, and a Brand Platform and Promise. This distinctive Brand DNA is the foundation that guides the strategy, development and evolution of the brand. It also guides the creation of internal processes, the cultivation of culture and leadership development required to bring a brand to life and support what it stands for. The Brand DNA creates the context for building an authentic brand.

With the above said we can't thank our clients enough for their trust in us and for allowing us to be their partner of choice in the elevation and evolution of their brands. We are thrilled at their dedication to embracing the Brand DNA process and applying conscious branding practices—where every employee thought, every action, and every interaction within the business supports and reaffirms the authenticity of what their brand stands for. We have learned so much along the way from each of them that we are now sharing this methodology with the world to help small and medium-sized businesses in their quest to build an authentic brand.

We want to thank Dr. Joseph Michelli, international speaker, author, and business consultant, for his insights, enthusiasm, and support for the work that we do and for inspiring his circle of influence to organizations that desire to be the best brands they can be.

We have been very fortunate to attend T. Harv Eker's Peak Potentials seminars, which literally gave us an innovative perspective in growing and building our brand consulting/training business and confidence in the unique approach we've developed to help other businesses walk their talk.

We want to thank the many people who reviewed the content and context of this book before it was in final form and gave us valuable feedback and meaningful testimonials. We are indebted.

And last but not least, we want to thank one of our primary editors, Sue Hamilton of Dialogue Publishing, for her insights, expertise, and support in bringing this book to print, and also our corporate attorney, Brenda Speer, who specializes in helping those in the creative arts express themselves and protect their inventions and the authorship of their own works.

# Preface

Meg walks through the door of her office on Monday morning with a glazed look in her eyes. Within ten minutes, her cell phone beeps with the first alarm notice of an upcoming conference call in fifteen minutes as seventy-four e-mails are downloading into her inbox. Once again, the weekend wasn't long enough and exists only as a blur in her memory.

Like Meg, you are a dedicated business entrepreneur; addicted to work. You spend numerous hours doing what you love or at least part of what you love. Your work is nonstop, with the e-mail, phone, fax, cell phone, the customer requests and complaints, making your payroll and managing your employees, paying your taxes, learning new technology, training, marketing campaigns, social networking, and strategic planning for global expansion. And you wonder why you are stressed. You think that if you tackle one more e-mail, one more task, and get them off your plate, you will feel better. Yet there is always one more e-mail, one more task; running the business is never ending. Your mind races at night while you toss and turn for several hours while thinking of more ways to capture market share, streamline production, and become more profitable. The constant drain affects your energy level, your health, and your state of mind, not to mention your productivity, so you end up working more hours—more than anyone else!

Lately, you've been relying on Starbucks® to get you going and keep you going. It offers a quick shot of caffeine right to the bloodstream, a real adrenaline high. What would you do without that caffeine? You can't hide from the realities of growing a business in a global economy today. You have special challenges. You are growing, and that growth adds new challenges daily. With these challenges come new responsibilities associated with growing your business brand. You are challenged with solving more complex problems like sourcing and hiring the right people who fit your brand, abandoning old ways of getting things done to get ahead of the curve, being more and more innovative and creative, and exploring new and leading-edge technology with a bit of trepidation. And you thought this was supposed to be fun.

To keep up and stay ahead of the competitive curve, staying innovative is vital. Courses and training are almost prohibitive due to time constraints and accessibility. Another hurdle is being sure that the educational program you select will get you the biggest bang for your buck. So how do you get to where you want to be in your business? When will you know that you've finally arrived? Consider the fact that growing your business is not about getting to the end goal. It is about the journey itself and what and how you learn and grow along the way. Building a business is never done.

Does this sound familiar? You are a small-business entrepreneur subjected to the same cycle over and over and over again. You are challenged with time, money, resources, legislation, and employee and customer needs to build your brand. Why is this? Well, it is because you don't know everything, and you don't expect yourself to. But you are smart and you are reading this right now, which means that you are seeking to learn and grow and be the best at whatever you challenge yourself to. You'd like to believe that if you work hard enough for long enough and come into a bit of luck, you'll strike gold. Confidence, skills, and passion are foundationally important, but there's more to building and positioning a highly successful business brand in our current competitive environment. Here are some interesting stats to consider.

## Small Biz Stats and Trends

The small-business marketplace continues to change rapidly. The information below represents the most current information as of this writing.

The estimated 27.2 million small businesses (defined as a business with fewer than five hundred employees) in the United States[1]:

- Employ about half of the country's private sector workforce
- Include 52 percent home-based businesses and 2 percent franchises
- Represent 97.3 percent of all the exporters of goods
- Represent 99.7 percent of all employer firms

- Generate a majority of the innovations that come from U.S. companies

Moreover, take a look at the following data on women-owned firms[2]:

- Women-owned firms produce employment for more than twenty-three million people in the United States, or 16 percent of our 2008 workforce.
- Approximately 8 percent of the total labor force works directly for a woman-owned firm.
- If U.S.–based women-owned businesses were their own country, they would have a greater GDP than Canada, India, and Vietnam combined.

For those of you reading this book who is involved with male-owned businesses, the above information is powerful for you in that it can help you to better understand the need to begin to understand the ever-expanding women-owned-business population and the opportunities available to create B2B relationships, partnerships, and alliances to further your own business growth goals.

## Small Business Survival Rates and Small Business Openings and Closings in 2007[3]

- There were 637,100 new businesses, 560,300 business closures, and 28,322 bankruptcies.
- Two-thirds of new employer firms survive at least two years, 44 percent survive at least four years, and 31 percent survive at least seven years.

Knowing that your business is contributing to these powerful statistics, the question becomes, "So where do you go from here?" There are so many choices, so many directions in which you can take your business. What do you focus on to get the most bang for your buck and time? How do you define, streamline, control, and strategize the evolution of your brand? What differentiators can you truly leverage? How can you be more consistent and relevant to your market? Who is your market? What's your brand's promise?

With all the pressures small-business entrepreneurs like you have, how can anyone expect you to stop, for a moment in time, and begin a structured process for investing time in the development of your core brand? There is something revealing about the old adage "ready, aim, fire" that often mimics how businesses are started. The goal is to "get the thing up and running smoothly as soon as possible so I can sit back and make a living," right? If it were just that easy! Your customers (including you) are both unconsciously and consciously seeking a return to the human element in our everyday transactions. Our rapid pace and unrelenting technology innovations (e.g., Twitter®, LinkedIn®, Facebook®, Plaxo®, MySpace®, etc.) penetrate our daily lives and blind our deep-seated needs to relate to human beings one on one, reaching into the emotional levels, creating meaningful relationships, trust, and consistency. This book and methodology help driven entrepreneurs refocus on the human element and reintroduce it into business strategy as it has lost its place among the focus on logistics, ROI, market reach, profit-and-loss reports, budgets, financial analyses, and bottom lines.

The Brand DNA methodology, outlined in this book through Meg's eyes, is a powerful gift to you—a gift that is not taught in business schools (yet), and a gift that will create a paradigm shift for your business in how you navigate the journey of defining, creating, and building your authentic business brand from the inside out.

View this book as if you were taking a course in brand building, share it with your employee team (if you have employees), and complete the exercises thoughtfully and creatively. If you are a solo-preneur, request the feedback from those who are invested in your success as a small business. Sharing the activities and outputs with your team or your selected support circle is a powerful component of digging deep to define your authentic brand, and the results will be exponential.

# PART I
# MEG'S WORLD

# Introduction: Meet Meg

Welcome to Meg's world. A budding entrepreneur passionate about the business she "birthed" three years ago, Meg was like many other entrepreneurs who had a great idea with a strong desire to build a business and be their own boss. Meg decided to take the plunge three and a half years ago, leaving a secure corporate role and venturing into the challenging world of entrepreneurism.

She had a window of opportunity when the company she worked for (an international, full-service, real estate development company) merged with another major player in the industry, leaving her with two choices: a move from her home in Denver to New York (their new corporate headquarters) or the option to take a severance package. Needless to say, she was in heaven. The timing couldn't have been better. It was a dream come true to take that severance package, cut the corporate cord, cash out her stock options, and start the business she had planned over the last year and a half.

She had enough in savings to manage her personal expenses for a while. Friends and family were ecstatic and offered to invest in the business, which she gladly accepted. She had enough cash to start but needed support both financially and emotionally to get her plan going.

With her former job, she obtained "platinum level" frequent-flier status three years running, traveling extensively throughout Asia Pacific and Europe. Back then, she spent more time traipsing through airports and meetings abroad with property investors and owners than in her office and home in Denver. The travel had its advantages and disadvantages. As a project manager, she was responsible for major construction and design projects around the world in their hotel and resort division, and she experienced many wonderful, exciting, and exotic places. Meg enjoyed some of the finest hotels and resorts around the globe.

With those experiences, she developed a great affinity for those resorts with the best spa treatments and would avail herself of those services whenever she could. She was especially fond of the resort treatments that used natural and organic products. Meg always knew when the products weren't authentically natural and organic. Her exceptionally sensitive skin tipped her off with severe allergic reactions, and she would break out in a raging rash all over her body that would linger for days with dry, flaky, and itchy skin. Meg's childhood was riddled with allergic reactions to all sorts of products. Her mother had the same allergic reactions. Because of her history, Meg was always hypersensitive about educating herself on ingredients that she was not familiar with.

Over time she learned which body care treatments and products she could trust and questioned everyone she could to find their sources for the products. That's when she went on a mission during her travels and in the spare time between meetings and projects. She'd take short excursions to find different ecological products with ingredients that were organic … only pure and natural. When she did find the products with the right ingredients, she indulged in the opportunity to experience them, pamper herself, and take detailed notes.

She developed quite a list of sources for the right ingredients, such as olive oil, glycerin, and sea salts, especially from the Dead Sea, aromatic oils, rose petals, and lavender, and she brought samples back to Denver. She formulated her own concoction of hand and body lotions, soaps, and balms. She infused aromatherapy oils and natural herbs into her unique recipes.

Meg made the products and gave them to her friends and family to try. They were great holiday and any-occasion gifts and were soon a huge success. Everyone loved and raved about the products and told their friends. Soon she had a slew of requests. It was then that she realized that she truly had a gem of a product line and a viable business model in the making. She was so done with the corporate rat race, the travel, the demands, and the internal politics and was ready for a major career change. Now she could leave that life behind and with much inspiration and an independent nature achieve her goals with gusto.

The name of her new company, Ecologé, and her first product line, "Eco-Cleanse," was created in a brainstorming session with five other friends and family members. She was ecstatic at what they had come up with in a half a day. After extensive discussion on the philosophy behind her new start-up and the research on the study of environmental/natural eco-systems, the name Ecologé sprang up.

A graphic designer was next on Meg's list. She wanted to define a powerful visual element to represent her company as soon as possible, sort of a way to make it more "real" for her. A friend of a friend introduced her to an artist who did some graphic design on the side and would be willing to create a corporate identity package. A logo, a business card layout, stationery, product line design packaging, and a Web site layout were proposed and designed. She had no idea of the work involved and the cost to do it professionally. When all was said and done about $7,500 was allocated to this particular project phase.

By the time the acquisition shifted her corporate world, Meg had already mapped out a draft business plan for her basic line of natural/organic body-care products. Then the real work began. It was a true test of her courage to stay the course. She had no idea how time would fly as she was consumed with all the details of producing and marketing her products. It was an enormous task to research and attend trade shows, home shows, and craft shows, source the right partners to manufacture and package the product line, and figure out how to set up the distribution network commercially to major hotels and resorts and then to individuals through home-based social gatherings. It wasn't easy breaking into this saturated industry and cutting through the clutter of all the other product lines on the market.

Finally, she managed to land one major commercial client through her former company contacts. She already had the home-based shows underway. However, this commercial client put her on the map and they negotiated a great deal. She would have preferred a higher price, but she needed to break into the market, and she did so with a moderate pricing structure.

Meg could be described as frugal and savvy. She had made decisions based on her gut ever since she was a little girl. No challenge was too great. She saw challenges as the "spice of life" and looked forward to what they would teach her. She learned that tenet from her father, who had a small retail business in Atlanta and grew it to five stores. He always said, "Snooze, you lose. Trust your gut, honey. Don't delay a decision too long or you may lose that perfect opportunity."

Her father taught her a sense of independence. She learned things from him like how to change a tire, how to change her car's oil, how to hang pictures in the house, and how to handle basic plumbing repairs. His influence in her life was one of the major factors in her decision to start the business in the first place. He was a rock, and she followed in his footsteps in that way. Now she was a lone wolf trying to do everything. The more she thought about that rock, the more inspired and determined she became to be the rock that she always known her dad to be.

Meg knew that she needed to expand the business. The responsibility of taking on additional employee overhead was scary. After twelve months of doing it all herself, she gave in and hired a salesperson. She knew she had to do this to grow the business and leverage her capabilities into a global market.

Three years later she has three employees and continues to grow. Two are sales reps and one is an office manager. Guess what? Sales numbers have reached a plateau, and her forecasted numbers show her falling short of budget this year. She accepted that this was in part due to the recent economic downturn. A more significant factor was that her sales reps were not quite representing the business in a way that reflected what the Ecologé brand is all about in order to attract the right customers in the right markets. As she analyzed it, Meg realized she was not real clear herself. If she wasn't clear, then how could her employees represent the brand if she had not defined and communicated it properly?

The realization hit her like a ton of bricks. The climax of this realization came during a recent sales call. She joined one of her sales reps to present to a major prospect. Wow, what an eye opener! She found herself politely correcting her sales rep in front of the customer on key questions regarding the brand and service expectations and even had to articulate their adherence to specific production standards; a differentiator that she discovered was underutilized with her sales team among other key attributes of the brand.

All of a sudden she felt desperate and started to think about how the customer complaints had increased, mainly in the area of service response time with shipment delays. In some cases, major customer shipments were delayed by weeks. Product quality had slipped slowly from her production source. Products were shipped with torn labels and poor print quality that didn't reflect the image of her brand. She'd searched for months for a new production source but hadn't been able to find it at the right price. Just the other week she lost two loyal customers to another competitor. She knew that she couldn't continue this downward spiral. To sustain an increase to her operating costs and bring on new customers at her current pricing structure was a difficult proposition. Besides the unfortunate series of events and her working harder than ever with fourteen-hour days to get through all the issues, she was exhausted!

On the brighter side, Meg secured one major speaking engagement. It was her first hotel and resort conference on the topic of health and lifestyle. The invitation came on the heels of her first published article for a dermatology trade magazine. Her efforts to increase her exposure were starting to pay off.

Up until this point she had been selling her products wholesale. The next phase of her plan was to open a natural body-care boutique in the right location. If that went well, then she wanted to open more locations, preferably in major urban areas to start, and then expand globally to Asia and Europe. Big ideas, big plans!

But how could she grow the business when she was barely breaking even? She knew she needed to develop a brand strategy to position and grow the business. She also believed that she needed to gain even more exposure in the right markets, and that would involve putting together a more robust marketing plan.

Following that recent eye-opening experience with her sales rep and customer, she was more aware of the need to understand and convey what Ecologé is and how to distinguish it in the market. How could she build a plan to evolve the brand so she could begin to realize her growth objectives? She needed a structure, resources, and a better process to ensure that who she hired was a good fit for her brand. She desperately needed consistency throughout every aspect of the business. Then she would need to develop a training program for her sales reps and get crystal clear on what her brand stands for. How could she deliver the training program in different markets? How could she afford all the training and travel expenses? Where should she begin?

Meg's company had outgrown what the basic e-commerce program on her Web site could do for her. She desperately needed a more robust program for marketing her products over the Internet. She wasn't getting the Web traffic she hoped for at this stage of the business life cycle, nor was she penetrating the market in the way she needed to grow. In the previous year, she spent a whopping 20 percent of her revenues on marketing activities alone. She had no idea of the return on that investment, other than the fact she was now coming out of the red zone, according to her accountant. With the recent loss of a key customer, she suspected she'd be back in the red. She had reached critical mass and was searching for the solutions that would guide her in the direction toward working smarter, not harder. She wondered how she could leverage her presence on the Web and in some way measure all those efforts overall.

Like many business entrepreneurs, Meg had a lot going for her. She was savvy, personable, and approachable. With a determined mind, quick wit, and strong resolve, she was absolutely committed to build a brand with a solid foundation before she grew it too fast and lost control. She'd heard and seen too many horror stories of people who got in over their heads and then lost their shirts. Nope, that wouldn't happen to her. Now there was no turning back either. Good was not even good enough. Her brand had to be *great*! Continuously searching for new ideas and unique ways of doing things was her modus operandi; including new partnership opportunities and new contacts and relationships to leverage her resources to build the business. She had to be the best in her business category and lead the market with a vengeance. Why not shoot high? If she didn't aim high she would never reach high. She savored the challenge.

She heard about a Webinar from a former colleague who forwarded it over e-mail: *Cashing in on Your Brand: Learn the secrets of conscious branding strategies and grow your business exponentially!* This free Webinar was sponsored by one of those major online conference providers and facilitated by the Brand Ascension Group (BA Group).

She was so intrigued that she signed up immediately in hopes that this would be the different approach that she was looking for. Because of her curiosity, she researched the presenter bios and service expertise on the Web site provided in the Webinar announcement. The BA Group had published e-books and coauthored a best seller. Their credentials spoke volumes, and their unique approach on internal brand definition strategy seemed intriguing and extremely logical to her. In their careers they had faced the same types of challenges Meg faced right at this moment. They had stood on the precipice ready to explore the global market abyss just like her.

After the sixty-minute Webinar presentation, Meg emerged with a new awareness and motivation to pursue the definition and development of the Ecologé brand; this time, from the inside out. She immediately took advantage of an online drawing for a complimentary business assessment and consultation with the Brand Ascension Group. She was also excited to know that they were headquartered in Colorado about sixty-five miles south of Denver, in Colorado Springs. Within a few days, she got a personal phone call from them informing her that she had been selected as the winner. She was thrilled at the opportunity and couldn't wait to find out the next steps, how soon, and where it would take place. The consultation was set near the end of the month.

The Brand Ascension Group sent Meg several brand-assessment tools to complete and return prior to the initial meeting. The assessment questions were very interesting and gave her much to think about.

Finally, the day arrived. At the start of the meeting, there was a bit of trepidation in Meg's voice as she sat with Suzanne Tulien and Carol Chapman around a circular granite table in a modern yet minimalist conference room in a newly renovated office building in Colorado Springs. They congratulated Meg on her win and gave a brief overview of their consulting and training practice as they served Starbucks® coffee and chocolate almond biscotti. Then they delved into the results of the assessment tools, which showed that Meg was doing the right things in certain areas but needed improvement in others. Some of the results astounded Meg, because she had never thought about the questions before. It led to a number of "Ahas" for her that begged even more questions. The Brand Ascension Group took the time to review and discuss with Meg their initial recommendations based on her results.

Meg gave an introduction and recounted her story over the last three years. The consultation was informal and conversational. In the dialogue back and forth, she let it all out. The encounter with the Brand Ascension Group was warm, focused, and engaging. The conversation was comfortably fluid and invigorating. They expressed tremendous empathy for the challenges Meg had faced over the last few years with her business. It was all so surreal. She could feel the excitement building, as visions of her future business growth began to take shape.

Four hours later, Meg knew she didn't know as much as she thought she did about defining and building a great business; or a great brand for that matter. *Great* didn't necessarily equate to biggest in size but rather to the realization of who and what the brand is and consistently behaving congruent to what her brand truly stands for. It is about defining the brand from the inside out and building actions and behaviors that are congruent and consistent, and then they (customers) will come. Meg had to believe. Building a great business and brand was about creating a set of principles to guide every thought and action, every interaction, and upholding herself and her employees to those same principles. True brand greatness is all about leveraging your unique brand attributes, organizing and defining the brand, and then creating and building a distinctive experience through processes and behaviors that create consistency and relevancy.

Meg learned a lot from that meeting; so much so that she committed to retain their services. They had one requirement: that she stays the course. They were insistent that branding is a process, not an event. She had to understand that building a business didn't happen in one event, like the creation of a logo or the launch of a marketing campaign. It was a continuous, evolving journey encompassing every facet of the organization. As the meeting wrapped up, the Brand Ascension Group narrowed down the focus to four critical phases—define, assess, build, and manage—in elevating the future of the Ecologé brand.

And the journey of Meg's Ecologé brand evolution began.

# CHAPTER 1

## Myth: My Brand is My Logo

*Nothing seems more obvious to me than a product or
service only becomes a brand when it is imbued with
profound values that translate into fact and feeling that
employees can project and customers can embrace.*
—*Richard Branson, CEO Virgin Airways*

## THE CHALLENGE

As I stepped out of the frigid temperatures into the warm, toasty
environment of the store, all my senses were at attention. I was fully
immersed in the scent of aroma-rich espresso and pastries in the air and
the soft sound of jazz music in the background. It was 7:30 AM. I exhaled
a deep breath and looked around to see a place full of people. Everyone
seemed fully engrossed in their moments of enjoyment. I spied Meg in a
corner, sitting in an overstuffed couch. She looked up; a big grin from ear
to ear emerged as she waved me over.

"Hi Carol," she said after she finished a gulp from her coffee and stood
up to greet me with a firm handshake.

"Hello Meg!" I said and then set my computer bag on the rectangular
coffee table while plunging into the soft overstuffed chair next to Meg.
"I just got off the phone with Suzanne. She's just around the corner," I
reassured.

"Great! I can't thank you enough for agreeing to meet here before we
begin today's Brand DNA session. I have a few things I need to share with
you and Suzanne that involve some immediate decisions for the business.
I couldn't think of a better place than this to grab some time before we
start our session," Meg remarked in an appreciative tone.

"Absolutely! I guess that's why they call it the "third place" after home
and office. You don't have to twist my arm to get me here," I replied.

"Me either. It's hard for me to pass up a Starbucks," said Meg.

"Well, now that you mention it, Starbucks is a wonderful example of what building a brand is all about!" I added. "Besides, the location is great. A quick walk under the viaduct and we're at BA Group's offices."

Meg shared a big grin, slapped her hand on her tote bag, and said, "I can't wait to show you what I have here. And what timing—there's Suzanne." She gestured her over with a warm welcome.

"Hello ladies! Brisk enough outside for you? Brrr, I need some coffee!" Suzanne said, setting her computer bag on the coffee table, ready to charge to the counter.

"Oh no, please; it's truly my treat! I insist. What would you both like?" Meg asked.

"Okay, you're on. How about a grande vanilla, soy chai latte?" Suzanne answered.

"I'll have a venti dry cappuccino with a touch of chocolate and cinnamon powder on top," I quickly added, almost too eagerly. Suzanne relaxed on the sofa next to Meg's spot. She and I conferred for a couple minutes regarding the Brand DNA session while Meg crossed over to the counter.

Meg was back in a flash. "Today's session will be a real pivotal point for Ecologé as it sparks the beginning of the defining moments of the future of your brand," I said.

"Well, I have to admit that my team and I have been in suspense for the last few weeks in anticipation of this session and what it will mean for our brand. We need to work on finding ways to market and sell more business, since we've lost some good customers recently and we're falling short of our revenue goals," she explained as she began to sift through her tote.

Immediately a red flag went up in my mind. "To clarify, Meg, today's session is not about exploring more ways to market or sell more business but rather to define the unique assets of the Ecologé brand," I explained.

"Oh, yes. I remember us talking about this session and the expected outcomes," she said as she pulled out a portfolio. Meg's face beamed with enthusiasm and eagerness. "Here we go! Tah dah!!" She placed and updated logo and business card design (Figure 1.1) on the table.

Figure 1.1

Suzanne and I looked at one another and then back to Meg, allowing her a bit more indulgence in the moment.

Meg bulldozed through, "I had two of my staff members, Kyla and Stefan, review the modifications and provide some input on the revisions before finalizing these. Aren't these cool? Oh and I have some great new ideas on my marketing brochure with a couple of new mock-ups that I want to show you today. Here they are! We have done a great job updating the information with a new exciting message about our brand and our products and services." Meg proudly displayed her new creative ideas. Her explosive energy bounced off the walls. "I'm so excited about this revised logo and the new brochure look and feel. I know this is the answer to get more business in the door. A fresh new look!"

"A quick question: how many times have you reworked your logo and changed the marketing message in your brochure since you started the business, Meg?" asked Suzanne innocently.

"Hmmm …" As Meg reflected and rubbed her chin, Suzanne cast a quick glance my way, lifting her eyebrow. Meg responded, "Well, probably on average … once, maybe twice a year. Umm … four or five times total in the last three years? Why do you ask?"

Suzanne asked another question, "Why have you had to rework the logo and brochure so many times?"

Meg took a deep breath and said. "Well, they didn't seem to be working for us. And I've never been satisfied with the logo look and feel, so we've continued to tweak it … because after all my logo is my brand!"

"Whoa," I said. "Your logo is your brand?"

"Meg," Suzanne asked, "What is the Ecologé brand? How do you define your brand?"

Meg thought for a minute and asked, "Is this a trick question?"

"Oh, no," said Suzanne.

"Well, my brand is what you see here in these materials, my logo mainly ... yes, isn't it?" asked Meg looking for approval.

Suzanne and I glanced yet again at one another and smiled.

I cleared my throat and replied, "Not exactly, Meg. Your logo is an important element of your brand that contributes in part to how others in the market perceive your brand. Your logo is merely a visual representation of the brand ... so that continues to beg the question: 'What is your brand?' That's the purpose of today's Brand DNA session. To help you clarify how you want to be perceived and what you stand for."

"The logo is only one element," Suzanne explained. "Your brand is much more than that. If you were to ask your customers what one or two words do you own in the minds of your market, what would they say?"

Meg pondered a few moments, "I think they would say pure and natural."

I asked, "Meg, how do you want them to define it; what do you want them to say?"

Meg sighed, "I want them to see us as simple and pure definitely, but other than that I'm not sure. I'm not really clear."

Suzanne responded, "This begs a further question that I want you to think carefully about. Do you think that because you are not clear this might be why you keep tweaking your logo and brochure?"

Meg's face turned beet red as she stumbled for words. She seemed a bit tense now. "I think you're trying to tell me something here, aren't you?"

"You've just admitted you are not clear on how you define your brand. And if you are not clear, how the heck do you expect your employees and customers to be clear on what the brand stands for?" Suzanne asked.

"Meg, can we take a step back for a moment? Would that be okay?" I asked.

"Sure," she replied.

"Thank you. In our last conversation we discussed some of the issues you were experiencing in the business, in particular inconsistencies in how your staff represent the brand and handle customers and service levels not meeting commitments you've made. Hence you've lost a few customers."

Meg flushed and put a hand to her forehead. "Oh yes. I do recall us talking about that."

Suzanne added, "Do you honestly think that further changes to the logo and brochure at this time will solve those issues?"

Meg thought about it for a moment and then replied. "I guess not. I know I need to work on the service issues, but how is defining my Brand

DNA going to help me do that? The logo and brochure are the most tangible things I have right now. I'm falling short of my revenue goals to date. I know this may look like a knee-jerk reaction. But I guess I'm not getting to the root of the issue, am I?"

It was clear we had some further educating to do to help Meg understand that building her brand was much more than a marketing exercise.

Suzanne scanned the room and said to Meg, "Look around you. What do you sense about this place? When you think of Starbucks (lifting up the coffee cup with the logo clearly in view) what comes to mind?"

Meg looked carefully around and said, "I see a lot of people enjoying themselves, doing their thing. I see employees having fun in the process of doing their jobs. It shows on their faces and in their laughter and conversations with customers. People are inspired when they come here. The place is tantalizing to all the senses. I love the environment; it makes me feel …" Meg stopped in mid-sentence. She looked at Suzanne and me with wide eyes and with her hand to her mouth mumbled, "I didn't say anything about the logo, did I?"

I shook my head, saying, "Nope! It is not about the logo or the brochure now, is it? You see the logo … it leaves an impression in your mind, but in and of itself it doesn't create the sole connection you have to the brand. It is not the green, black, and white colors in the logo with an illustration of a sea witch that keeps you coming back into this establishment, is it? Of course not! It's the experience you have when you come to Starbucks that creates the emotional connection that you bond with. The logo merely represents that emotive feeling and helps you to identify where you can get that connection, but that's all. Starbucks is much more than its logo. The Ecologé brand is much more than its logo."

Suzanne added, "So how do you expect your logo and brochure in and of itself to address the service issues with your staff and to create the connection you want your customers to have with the Ecologé brand?"

Meg was in deep thought, taking it all in.

Suzanne continued, "It's the experience that your customers have that creates the connection to your brand. It's the unique style in which you present the brand. It's the behaviors and way you do business, the values your brand stands for, and how your customers perceive you relative to those values. That's why you need to work on the foundational components of the brand. Defining your Brand DNA through our step-by step process will establish and guide the experience you want to deliver for your customers and for your employees as well. It will help you address the service issues and how employees represent your brand."

"The definition of your Brand DNA is the missing piece your brand has been lacking since you started the business," I said. "Don't get me wrong—you've done well so far, but you can take this business a lot farther. However, you keep spinning your wheels by refining your logo and brochure when what you need to think about is putting a stake in the ground. You need to get crystal clear on *what* the Ecologé brand stands for, how you want to show up, how you want your customers to feel, and what you want to own in the minds of your customers."

Suzanne leaned closer toward Meg and added, "The Brand DNA session takes you and your team through a discovery process of the four critical components that distinguish you from others in the market … *your values, your style, your standards, and your differentiators,* all of which set you apart, and which no one else does better than the Ecologé brand!"

"Exactly," I said. "And from these components you and your team will extract and develop your Brand Platform and Promise, all of which set the guiding rules for doing business. Why do you think Starbucks is so successful? Is it because of the pretty green and black sea witch?" I pointed at the logo on the coffee cup.

"No, definitely not!" said Meg.

I added, "Ahh … we're making some progress. It's because Starbucks has defined the critical elements of their brand attributes, and they deliver on these elements, day in and day out."

"One cup at a time," Suzanne added. "Starbucks can't deliver the way they do without communicating the values upon which the brand was created. It can't deliver without creating the systems and processes and cultivating the culture that supports their values. And neither can a lot of other highly successful brands like Disney, Nordstrom, Ritz Carlton, Southwest Airlines, Virgin, Harley-Davidson, GE, Johnson & Johnson, and Bath & Body Works. Need we go on?"

Meg sighed and sunk back into her cushioned seat. "Wow! I have a lot to learn from the two of you. Where has my head been? This seems like the most obvious thing now, but I couldn't see it before. It's going to take some work to retrain my brain in how I think about my brand and where I focus my time, energy, and money."

I put my hand on Meg's shoulder and said, "Relax! Do you think you're the first entrepreneur who has gotten caught up in the trap of believing your logo is your brand and that's what branding is all about?"

Meg smiled and said, "I can see now how my brand is so much more than the logo but rather is the attributes that define our DNA."

Suzanne reinforced, "And that's why you and your team need to create the foundation that guides the experience you want to create by defining the details of Ecologé's Brand DNA."

"So the DNA will help guide me in my efforts like Starbucks has done?" asked Meg.

"Absolutely! It will lay the foundation for creating the road map to elevate your brand. Once we get through the next two days of the Brand DNA session you will be clear on what your brand stands for and have a much better foundation for elevating the brand. So do you see how it would be highly beneficial for you and your team to work on the foundational components of your brand before you redesign the logo and create any new messages?"

"Yes," Meg said.

"All right then; are you ready to get started?" asked Suzanne.

Meg replied with a definitive, "Yes!"

"Okay, let's head to the office," I said.

Meg, Suzanne, and I entered the meeting room just outside the reception lobby of the floor that held the Brand Ascension Group offices. My assistant, Sharon, had everything ready to go: digital light projector, laptop, screen, workbooks, and refreshments for the three of us and the five people who already sat casually around the large conference room table. Our invitees to this critical session were Meg's team of three: her office manager, Kyla; her East Coast sales rep, Sadie; and her West Coast sales rep, Stefan. All had been hired within the past eighteen months. Leeza, a close friend of Meg's and an avid supporter of the brand, and Ty, a former colleague, were on hand, too. We all made our introductions and the session began.

We started with an experiential ice breaker: *Who's on Your Team.* This exercise helps the team understand that one of the key elements to building a successful brand involves trust within the team. Trust is the foundation of every successful relationship. It is one person to another. It starts with getting to know who is on your team and their interests and talents both on a personal and a professional level. We also shared several stories of enduring brands to demonstrate a common thread within all these brands—core values. Suzanne and I challenged the group to think about the Ecologé brand's core values. "These are the core principles that are essential to everything you do collectively as a brand; how you behave and act in the world in which you do business," Suzanne said.

"Why are values important?" I asked the group.

I then emphasized, "These values are why you say yes or no to a key decision that impacts the current state and ultimately the future of the business. Look into the future, ten years from now, and think about the magic story of Ecologé and the team of people who built it from the guiding principles that are at the heart of everything that makes the brand what is. What are those core values?"

"What is consistent and enduring in the history of the brand that forms the basis for who you are and what you represent?" asked Suzanne.

I could feel the energy in the room change. As Meg grabbed a juice from the back table she said, "We are authentic and pure and natural, and we don't claim to be any more than that, at least not yet; there may be more after today, right? We will always create products that are in harmony with the earth, are non-allergenic, and contain only the purest ingredients."

"Great start, but not too quick just yet," I said, cueing Suzanne. "You'll have plenty of time to answer that. We're planting the seeds of thought."

Suzanne said, "We're going to press ahead and speak about the style of the Ecologé brand next, so hold those thoughts. They're great thoughts." She walked to the white board and wrote the words: 'Style = Your Brand's Personality!' Then she said, "We also want you to think about the personality of the Ecologé brand ten years from now. What is it that continuously reflects the manner in which you do business? What is distinctive about the persona of the Ecologé brand in the minds of the market, in your minds? What makes you who you are? If Ecologé were a famous person, who would it be? Oprah, Audrey Hepburn, Ralph Lauren? They all have distinctive personality traits, right? So, how would you describe the personality of Ecologé? Think about that as we take a short break. When we come back you will dive deep in order to define and articulate the values and style attributes of the brand."

**SEE PART II: READER EXERCISES, CHAPTER 1 EXERCISE, for your BRAND VALUES AND STYLE exercises and ECOLOGE's final outputs.**

## CONSULTANTS' CORNER

Do you typically associate your brand with your logo? A lot of business owners and their teams do. It is a common misconception! They assume that once they design their logo, business card, marketing brochure, and Web site the branding is done. That couldn't be further from the truth.

Here's a great example:

Are YOU guilty of spending $4 for the brand experience of a Starbucks® cup of coffee when you can go to the local gas station and get it for $.99?

Is it because you like the colors green and black and have an affinity with the sea witch in the center? No, you buy it for the experience. It is the rich Italian espresso aroma, the comfortable environment, the soothing music, the convenience of the drive-thru, and the pleasant, friendly, and engaging personalities of the staff. Starbucks customers come back over and over again because of their positive experiences—a multisensory event that remains in their memories for the long term!

**Your Brand Is Much More Than Your Logo**

Your brand is a *perception* that is based on *emotion* and defined by the *experiences* of others with you, your products, and services.

So when you think about that experience, the brand becomes more than the logo in and of itself—the logo is simply a representation of the experience! The experience serves as an expression of your brand. See beyond the aesthetic look of your logo, signage, business cards, collateral, Web site, and advertisements. Your brand is expressed through how you live and embody its essence, as in:

- Deeply rooted *values* and how these show up authentically within the context of how you do business.
- A distinctive *personality* that reflects the manner in which you do business.
- A deepening *relationship* with your employees and customers and the bonding that occurs.
- The commitment to a *promise* to those you serve and the trust that grows.
- The unique *experience* with your brand and the loyalty that transpires.
- The *one word* or *concept* that you own in the mind of your market that endures the test of time.
- The *gestalt* (more than the sum of the parts) feeling that lingers in the minds of your market.

Meg's belief that her logo was the lifeblood of her brand and that an update to the logo and marketing collateral would solve her customer retention problems is a common reaction for most business owners. Because business owners don't take the time to define what their brand is all about and how they want to show up in the market, they continue to waste valuable dollars that in the end don't get to the root of their problems.

Business owners need to think about building trust with new and existing customers by delivering consistently on what they stand for as a brand. Consider these statistics on factors affecting customer loyalty:

According to Carlson Marketing[1], the top four reasons that drive customer loyalty, from a customer's point of view:

The company addressed mistakes—80 percent
Being treated well by company staff—75 percent
Companies made the extra effort—65 percent
Staff truly interested in them—60 percent

Think about these statistics the next time you lose a customer. What could you have done differently to retain their loyalty? Loyalty is the state of feeling attached to somebody or something. A certain trust and allegiance occurs when a customer is made to feel important, and the care exhibited is the kind that is felt when they are treated well. These statistics suggest some simple opportunities to ensure that you retain your customers. How difficult is it to address a mistake and make the situation right for your customer? How difficult is it to treat your customers like you would want to be treated? The next time you think about creating customer loyalty, don't start with a focus on your marketing. Start with a focus on internal aspects of your brand: hiring and training the right people, shaping a culture that reinforces what your brand is all about, and creating systems and processes that enable the delivery of brand experiences that truly reflect what you claim your brand to be in your marketing.

## Your Brand DNA (Dimensional Nucleic Assets®)

What is it? Your Brand DNA is the foundation that drives the creation of the overall brand experience. (See page 151 for a template of the Brand DNA model.) Your *Brand DNA,* or what we term your brand's *Dimensional Nucleic Assets®,* is the core characteristics and levers of competitive advantage unique to your brand. Like an individual's DNA, a brand's DNA is unique to it. It is the genetic code that guides the growth, development, and overall evolution of your brand. It guides how your employees behave, live, and embody the essence of your brand and sets the guiding rules for doing business.

Briefly, the first two critical components of your Brand's Dimensional Nucleic Assets are your *values* and *style*:

1. ***Values***—The guiding principles that reflect your core ideology. These principles are the foundation and are essential to everything you do for your customers and employees.

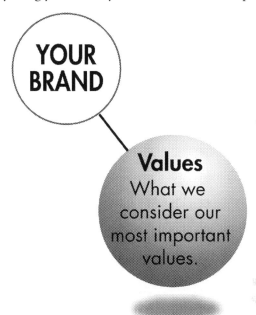

It is easy to talk about values. A lot of companies have invested numerous hours and lots of money to establish values only to store them on a shelf and never use them again. Worse yet, they are never exhibited in the actual behaviors of employees. There has to be a direct reflection of the words and their definitions in the behaviors of employees that reflect the brand. Otherwise, values are just lip service.

In the book *Built to Last*[2] by Jim Collins and Jerry Porras, Johnson & Johnson's credo (statement of belief) was reported as it was written in 1943 by R. W. Johnson Jr. Their credo is an example of an organization's values in action that have endured the test of time. The credo reflects a set of guiding principles from the era in which they were born. Although it has been slightly updated over time, Johnson & Johnson's employees have consistently lived the credo and the values it contains day in and day out. Their actions have become a part of the culture of the brand and have reflected the philosophy of the founders for many years.

Ultimately our actions say so much more than the words themselves on a piece of paper or hung on a wall. According to a global survey of 365 companies in thirty countries conducted by Booz Allen Hamilton and the Aspen Institute[3], the following are some key findings regarding organizations and values:

- Most companies believe values influence two important strategic areas—relationships and reputation.
- Top performers consciously connect values and operations. They are also more successful in linking values to the way they run their companies. A significantly greater number reported that their management practices are effective in fostering values that influence growth.
- A CEO's tone really matters, as 85 percent of the respondents said their companies rely on explicit CEO support to reinforce values.

Think about the values that form the basis of your brand. Have you articulated them, and if so, do you and your colleagues' actions reflect those values?

2. *Style*—Distinct manner in which you present and deliver your products and services; your brand's personality.

Think about your brand's personality. Are you a Cadillac or a Volkswagen, a Range Rover or a Honda? Why one over the other? How do you express your brand? How do your employees relate to one another, your customers, or your suppliers? What is distinctive about the expression of what your brand stands for? How does it come across in the actions that illustrate how the brand is lived? Is your style casual or sophisticated, understated or boisterous? Are you controlled or spontaneous? How about principled or pragmatic?

What determines the answers to these questions is how authentic any one of these style descriptions is to your actual brand and how consistent you are in portraying them. Think of this as a study of who you are and the perceptions of your employees of how you show up behaviorally both internally and externally. It is a fabulous exercise that gets to the foundational level of your brand and aids in the creation of the systems and processes that will affirm and reaffirm your brand in the minds of your customers at every touch point.

# CHAPTER 2

## *Myth: It's My Company; I Know Who I Am*

*You have to leave the city of your comfort and go into
the wilderness of your intuition. What you'll discover
will be wonderful. What you'll discover is yourself.*
*—Alan Alda*

## THE CHALLENGE

After breaking for lunch, we continued our Brand DNA session.

"With today's high-tech, low-touch society, 'sensory branding' may be the only way back to a human-centered environment"[1] said Suzanne, emphasizing a quote on a PowerPoint slide. I then stepped over to a flip chart with a marker and in a slow, deliberate movement with my hand wrote down two words. When I finished, I asked, pointing to the flip chart, "What does human-centered mean?"

Meg, the first to provide an answer, said with an uncertain inflection in her voice halfway between a statement and a question, "Isn't it about appealing to who we are as human beings? Understanding and being in tune with others' needs, creating a warm feeling that lets people know we care?"

I replied, "Ahh, very good. And how do we let people know we care?"

"By leaving such a positive and memorable impression and making them feel really important?" asked Meg.

"Good again. How do we create an impression?" I asked as I moved to the other side of the room, gesturing with my arms outward to engage the rest of the group in the discussion.

Sadie responded, "It's how we interact with our customers, how we service them, and how attentive we are."

"Absolutely," I said, "But how do we ensure that type of impression?"

Ty spoke up, "By being consistent in those interactions and by ensuring consistency in products and service delivery."

Suzanne leaned against the table and said, "Yes, consistency is key to how we show up and is essential to leaving a lasting positive impression. Let me ask this: how do we as humans perceive?" she questioned, trying to elicit more understanding within the group.

There was a long pause and a couple of perplexed looks, wondering where she was going with the conversation. Suzanne clicked the remote, and up popped six little graphics on the screen: a person's eye, an ear, a nose, a mouth, a handshake, and a forehead with a circular symbol on it.

"Oh, through our senses," Kyla blurted out. "Duh!"

"And that's how we create an impression, by appealing to the senses of sight, sound, taste, touch, smell, and intuition. As human beings, we take in thousands of bits of information through all the senses. That's what is meant by sensory branding through a human-centered environment," I said. By then, everyone was nodding their heads in understanding. It had started to click.

Suzanne and I glanced briefly at each other with smiles, ever so amazed by the "Ahas" our clients experience every time we facilitate this session. Simple examples that articulate the point in subtle yet reflective ways enabled Meg and the group to better understand what they were experiencing and learning in this session.

"By capitalizing on multisensory experiences and 'out-behaving' your competitors, you can leave a lasting, favorable impression in the minds of your market. You can distinguish yourselves to be that ever-sought-after brand of choice among your customers," said Suzanne.

"Can you give us some specific examples?" asked Stefan as he scratched his head.

Suzanne replied, "By demonstrating more care and commitment to one another and your customers, by being more responsive to your customers' needs, and by taking the time to nurture your customers. What else?" she gestured back to the group for their input.

Meg offered, "By responding quickly to their requests; by creating 'Wow' experiences at every point of contact with a customer, whether through e-mail, a phone call, a personalized letter, or through the delivery of our products, our packaging—everything. We have so many opportunities!"

"Think about all the touch points and the opportunities to leave a lasting and memorable impression," reaffirmed Suzanne. "Being conscious about your brand is the key to managing it. Always put yourself in your customers' shoes and experience your business through their eyes, ears, noses, etc."

I could see more "Ahas" in the eyes of the group. I added, "And by establishing standards of performance that create a level of excellence in what you do and that you adhere to day in and day out to ensure the consistency of that experience through all the senses."

Suzanne looked at Meg and her three team members directly and said, "Your brand standards will help you identify and create policies and procedures that empower each of you to 'Wow' the customers, exceed their expectations, resolve issues, think creatively, and share ideas that enhance and affirm at every opportunity the overall experience of the brand."

There was a long pause as I glanced briefly at each person around the table and then fired off a few compelling questions. "How many of you want the Ecologé brand to make people feel important and special? Raise your hand!" I put mine in the air. "How many of you want your customers to do even more business but only with you?" The entire group raised their hands indicating a unanimous "yes." "That's why you're here!"

Suzanne then asked, "Are you the talk of the industry? Is everyone knocking on your doors for the experience? How do you create something so unique that everyone will want to be a part of it and tell their friends, family, and colleagues?"

"By delivering to our customers in exceptional ways that they don't experience elsewhere?" asked Meg.

"Yes, and by knowing what sets you apart. By getting clear on what your brand stands for and leveraging the heck out of it," Suzanne answered.

Gesturing to the flip charts on the wall, I said, "Earlier this morning we delved into your style attributes and values. And as a result of the exercise, here is what you came up with:

**Style Attributes**
*chic, avant-garde, personable, savvy*
**Values**
*environmentally conscious, purity, simplicity, harmony*

"These are very distinctive and have great potential for creating actionable behaviors that you as a team can invent to ensure that the Ecologé brand is consistent in these attributes at every touch point externally and internally within your employee culture. Now let's discover what the

Ecologé brand's unique differentiators and standards are. But first let's cover the definition of each."

Suzanne clicked the remote to the next slide on the screen. A graphic and the word *"DIFFERENTIATOR"* popped up. She explained, "The differentiators of Ecologé are your unique and distinctive capabilities that enhance what you bring to the business and your customers. They represent and confirm that you are experts in your industry and the respective markets in which you do business."

"What if we haven't truly identified and leveraged what we can be the best at or even communicated to our customers what differentiates us?" Meg asked.

"Oh wow, this is such an eye opener," interjected Leeza. "We have so many opportunities that we haven't taken advantage of. One of the things we have talked about is to create more personalized distribution and service to our customers. We've researched the best sources of eco-friendly and hypoallergenic ingredients and their healing and relaxation properties. We created a unique line of imported botanicals. We need to work on communicating and leveraging our differences."

"What about those you contract with to produce the special compounds of your products? Are they certified or licensed in specialized areas of biochemistry, dermatology, or organics?" inquired Suzanne.

Meg replied, "Oh, here's a differentiator. We have partnered with the Phoenix Research Center, which has certified botanists, biochemists, dermatologists, and biologists on staff. They have also won all sorts of awards in their fields. All of our products are specially crafted, blended, and tested for their healing and therapeutic properties. Every product must go through a rigorous analysis and testing process before we make a decision to include it in our line."

"And we thought we knew our company!" interjected Stefan. "Now that we are doing a deeper dive into what we are, we are tapping into the true uniqueness that exposes our competitive advantage. I don't think I would have thought of our brand in this way without this probing discussion. Let's keep going with the ideas."

Suzanne raised her right index finger and said, "And you will, as a team, collaborate on generating more ideas today. But first let's talk about another aspect of the Dimensional Nucleic Assets process, which is your standards." She clicked the remote again to move to the next slide. "Anyone care to define what we mean by standards?" A graphic of four conjoining colored balls emerged on the screen.

This time, Leeza spoke up. "I would think it is a level of service that you maintain. For example, if you promise the customer that their order will be delivered within three to five days, then you need make sure that happens."

"And if we say we guarantee 100 percent satisfaction, then we bend over backward to make it right for the customer," piped in Meg.

"Exactly!" Suzanne reaffirmed. "It is that level of performance excellence to which you set the bar for yourselves at the internal and external levels." She clicked the remote again, and up popped four colored balls on the screen each with a word inside: *Employees, Customers, Processes, Financial.* "This is what we refer to as your Brand Scorecard (Figure 2.1)."

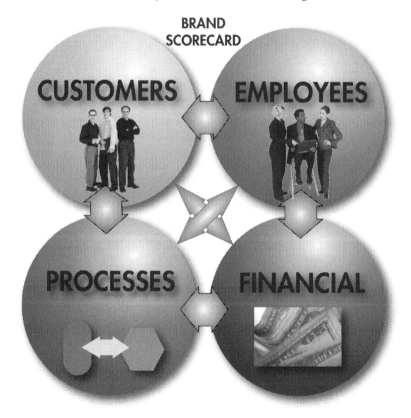

Figure 2.1

The group was nodding. I observed from their expressions that they were absorbing a lot.

Suzanne continued, "Focusing on these four key aspects of the business to establish standards will help direct your collective efforts, abilities, and resources toward achieving the long-term positioning of your brand. Adhering to standards will enable you to elevate the brand experience internally and externally, continually raising the bar so as to be consistent and distinctive."

"When you compose the overarching standard for each area of the brand scorecard, then you will be asking yourself to dig a bit deeper and identify four to six supportive actions that will serve to guide you and your team in ensuring that the standard is supported. These supportive actions are a great way to flesh out a step-by-step approach to make sure each of your standards is achievable and can be actionable."

"Here's the test," I said. "Does Ecologé guarantee 100 percent satisfaction to your customers, and do you deliver on that commitment every single time?" There were a couple of head shakes that suggested "no."

Meg stood up to stretch her legs and continued, "Well, we have had some issues, mainly because some of our vendors were not meeting their commitments. That reflects negatively on us in the eyes of our customers. Many of the ingredients in our products are imported from Asia and Europe. Sometimes delivery schedules can vary depending on the area. Some of this is out of our control, and we're working on establishing more rigorous standards requirements for our vendors. What's in our control is how we respond to our customers. Right now we're not consistent in that response. We need to follow up with every customer consistently. We need to define what personalized service translates to in how Ecologé delivers to our customers from initial order to shipment received to invoicing to thank-you notes and gifts that show our appreciation for their business. At a minimum, when there is an issue we should follow up with a personal phone call to let them know that we care and we are working to make the situation right. In fact, we need to be more proactive by identifying if there is an issue in delivery before they find out about it. That gives us the opportunity to do what it takes before it affects them or reflects negatively on us."

"So would you agree that how you respond through your behavior and your actions is a moment of truth in the mind of the customer?" I asked. Everyone nodded in agreement.

"Absolutely! Let's take a short break. Come back in ten minutes and we'll break you into two groups to work on identifying your differentiators and standards," instructed Suzanne.

**SEE PART II: READER EXERCISES, CHAPTER 2 EXERCISE, for your DIFFERENTIATORS and STANDARDS exercise and ECOLOGE's final outputs.**

# CONSULTANTS' CORNER

Have you taken the time to think through and examine the distinctive characteristics and capabilities that enhance what you bring to your business and your customers? Think about what you provide in terms of your products and services. Consider the following questions. What answers do these trigger in your mind?

1. What distinguishing capabilities set you apart from others in your industry?
2. Do you see training as important and necessary? Do you invest an appropriate portion of time and dollars into staff training—above and beyond your competitors?
3. Do you take the time to acknowledge and celebrate your "wins" with your staff?
4. Do you have a profit pool or "win-win" system for your staff to be acknowledged?
5. Do you have a unique service model?
6. Do you have processes that enable you to more spontaneously and effectively service your customers compared to your competitors?
7. Do you have a state-of-the-art technology or methodology that no one else can duplicate?
8. Do you offer a "one-stop" shopping experience with seamless delivery?
9. Are you consistently the recipient of award-winning technologies, practices, services, etc., in your industry category?
10. Do you have intellectual capital or other trade secrets that no other competitor can claim they have or duplicate?
11. Do you have a one-of-a-kind, cost-effective approach to producing a product?

## YOUR BRAND DIFFERENTIATORS

These are the unique and distinctive capabilities that enhance what you bring to the business and your customers and what your expertise is within your industry and the respective markets in which you operate.

These are the types of capabilities that businesses of all sizes can leverage. Your distinctive capabilities can be a tremendous source of competitive advantage. Differentiation is a critical step if a brand is to set itself apart in the marketplace and occupy a distinctive position in the customer's mind.

Consider the following brands and how they have leveraged their distinctive attributes that create differentiation:

Build-A-Bear Workshop® (www.buildabear.com), an experiential retail store where the buyers construct their own stuffed bear using assorted accessories.

- Founded in 1997, it delivers memorable brand experiences through a highly experiential and interactive retail store environment.

- The stores are very distinctive and highly themed with lots of color. All the senses are tantalized, especially sight, sound, and touch.
- The bear-making process consists of several stations: Choose Me, Hear Me, Stitch Me, Fluff Me, Dress Me, Name Me, and Take Me Home. These stations take the customer through the entire bear-making experience.
- Store associates are referred to as Master Bear-Builder® associates. They interact with the customer, sharing and helping in their individual bear-making experience.
- At the Take Me Home station, each bear is provided with a birth certificate and a bar code is placed inside that identifies the owner if the toy is lost. A bear can be reunited with its owner if returned to any Build-A-Bear Workshop store.
- Guests can also go online to the Build-A-Bear Workshop Web site for a furry adventure and/or to purchase a new toy. It is a virtual experiential and fascinating online experience.

Harley-Davidson® (www.Harley-Davidson.com)
- One of its differentiators is the Harley Owners Group® (HOG®). The group sponsors rallies, road tours, festivals, touring handbooks, and all sorts of events celebrating the experience of the Harley owner/rider.
- Harley-Davidson has leveraged the power of its symbol by putting its brand on many products, such as clothing, accessories, and paraphernalia.
- Harley-Davidson motorcycles have maintained a distinctive look, feel, and sound, regardless of competitor design trends over the years.
- Harley-Davidson is persistent in the delivery of a distinguished level of service to its dealers and suppliers.

Hyperfit USA (www.hyperfitusa.com)
- One of their core beliefs is that people need to be successful with their fitness. They ascribe to CrossFit™—a core strength and conditioning training approach through general physical fitness supported with functional movements that are constantly varied and executed at high intensity.

- Hyperfit USA provides people with workout training that stretches their capacity along with a community of people who support one another.
- Hyperfit USA also provides benchmarking so members can gauge performance improvement over time.
- Its distinct fitness program is empirically driven, clinically tested, and community developed.
- Hyperfit USA is about delivering value. On their Web site, as of this writing, they have a list of ten reasons why *not* to join. Reason #1: They make you try out. Just having a credit card and pulse does not get you a membership.

## YOUR BRAND STANDARDS

Consider what would happen if the following happened to you as it actually did to a colleague of ours. You are running late for a meeting after a delayed lunch with a client. You realize that you forgot to make an important deposit into your bank account, which has to be in by 2:00 pm or it won't be credited until the next business day. It is 1:55 pm as you swing by the drive-thru window at your local branch. There is no line.

What luck, you say to yourself as you pull into an open stall and are greeted by a teller with, "I'm sorry, you'll have to wait, because we have customers in line inside, and they are our first priority."

You are absolutely taken aback by this teller's response, lack of sensitivity, and the apparent standard of the bank to allow this type of behavior. You wonder what kind of service level this is to be so bold as to blatantly admit to customers which ones are more important than others. You think, "If they have a drive-thru, why don't they have designated staff to manage and service it?"

Now think as an entrepreneur or a consumer and ask yourself, "Is this acceptable behavior? Is this an acceptable standard for customer treatment?" No, of course not. It turns out that it was not an acceptable standard for this bank but rather a training issue with a new hire. The company probably didn't take the time to assess the employee's customer service ethic during the hiring process. That specific behavior was the tipping point for making the decision to close the account and open a new one with the bank's competitor.

Your *brand standards* are levels of performance excellence across a Brand Scorecard[2] at the internal and external levels: employees, customers, processes, financial.

Many smaller businesses do NOT take the time to think about standards of performance, let alone establish them. Standards are the most tangible and measurable elements of your Brand DNA. Standards are a defined level of performance excellence across what we refer to as your Brand Scorecard: *employees, customers, processes, and financial.*

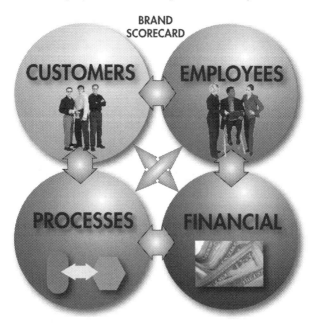

The scorecard reflects the quality and level of performance in how you do business and what metrics you establish for yourself. Your standards are a reflection of the strength in the substance of your brand and how you intend to set the bar and measure success against a set of criteria. Consider the following questions when thinking about what these standards might look like in your business:

**Employees**—What do you commit to in terms of who you hire, how you orient and train your people to follow through on what your brand represents, and what you will provide in return for their efforts? What supportive actions will need to be identified to ensure that you consistently achieve this established standard?

**Customers**—What level of performance excellence (in the products and services you provide, level of satisfaction, etc.) do you commit to consistently deliver to your customers? What supportive actions will need to be identified to ensure that you consistently achieve this established standard?

**Processes**—What level of excellence will you establish in your daily business operations related to your policies, procedures, and practices that reflect what your brand stands for? What supportive actions will need to be identified to ensure that you consistently achieve your established standard?

**Financial**—What level of returns or rewards will you establish for customers and investors, employees, and vendors that will make them want to be a part of your brand? What supportive actions will need to be identified to ensure that you consistently achieve your established standard?

For example, companies like Starbucks only hire and train great people that "fit" their brand. They hire those who are zealous about coffee and have passion and commitment to serve as true ambassadors for the coffee and the brand. They ensure that they hire people with a personal attachment to the brand and know how to connect with their customers to keep them coming back for more. In return, Starbucks refers to their employees as "partners." They introduced benefits for part-time employees, and everyone participates in their "bean stock" program as reported in *Pour Your Heart Into It*[3] by Howard Schultz, Chairman of Starbucks.

Customers at Wegmans Food Markets rank the ease of returning items higher than Nordstrom. Wegmans has created an exceptional standard for its return policy and received the best scores of any retailer on ease of returning.[4]

Zappos.com was founded in 1999. They finished 2009 at almost $1.2 billion in revenues. They moved to number fifteen on Fortune's 2010 100 Best Companies to Work For list. And a whopping 75 percent of purchases are from repeat customers! At Zappos.com, customer service is everything. In fact, it is the entire company.

Zappos.com Customer Standard[5]:

Provide the best customer service possible; internally that means "Wow" the customer at every touch point.

Supportive Actions:

- Free shipping—both ways (usually overnight).
- 365-day return policy (yes, up to a full year to return).
- 24/7 customer service .
- All new hires attend four weeks of customer loyalty training (answering phones in their call center) before starting the job they were hired for.
- Employee empowerment—do what it takes to wow their customers, because customer service is everyone's responsibility.

Now, when you think about your own overarching standards for your brand, consider what levels of performance excellence you will establish and adhere to.

# CHAPTER 3

## *Myth: My Tagline is My Brand Promise*

*My desire is for our product and message to capture
the imagination of our customers, to inspire them
toward a peaceful and fulfilling lifestyle, and to
provide them with a little dose of energy to persevere
and adjust through any time, good or bad.*

*—Bill Rosenzweig,
Co-founder of The Republic of Tea,
April 12, 1990*

## THE CHALLENGE

It was 9:03 AM on the second day of the Brand DNA session for Meg and her team.

As I turned the energizing music to pause, Suzanne opened the session with, "You all did a great job yesterday. Look at all this work." She pointed around the room at the array of colorful flip-chart pages taped to the walls and windows. "How do you feel about what you accomplished?"

The question was met with a number of resounding responses like "Let's keep going."

"Great!" she said. "Before we get started, let's do a quick review of yesterday's session. This is part of our regular review throughout our sessions following the 10/24/7 philosophy of a ten-minute review every twenty-four hours over a seven-day period to ensure retention of concepts, methods, and application. So grab a partner, walk around the room, and review the flip-chart notes and share with one another your understanding of the information we covered yesterday and what it means for the Ecologé brand going forward." The sound of voices in the room increased a few decibels as the group got up and did their sharing.

Within ten minutes, the group had settled back into their seats. "Any questions or comments regarding yesterday's session?" I asked.

Meg was the first to comment. "Only that we have a lot of work to do to begin implementing our Brand DNA, and I'm feeling elated yet also overwhelmed by what we accomplished yesterday. I'm wondering how we will make it all come together." She relaxed with her elbows resting on the table and her hands cupped to her chin.

I replied, "Your response is pretty common at this stage of the session. Most of our clients begin to feel a bit overwhelmed. You'll feel less so as we begin to get into the initial group exercises around how to operationalize what you've defined within your unique Brand DNA, which will occur during the latter half of today's session and in our follow-up sessions. Remember one thing: Branding is not a one-shot deal or a marketing event, as you've begun to realize. It is a strategic, deliberate, and conscious process of being consistent and true to what your brand is all about—every single day. All we ask is that you trust in the process and trust in yourselves. Can we agree to that?"

"Absolutely," replied Meg.

Suzanne then grabbed a blue marker and wrote on the flip chart Brand Platform. She turned to the group and said, "Let's explore what this is so that we can begin to create it for Ecologé. Your Brand Platform reflects the most dominant characteristics of your brand." She continued to write key words on the flip chart as she spoke, "It is your brand's *fundamental essence*, consistent across all *product categories and services,* and is derived from your most *distinctive attributes.* For it to be crisp and understandable it is described in three to four highly descriptive words.

Kyla raised her hand indicating a question. "I think we already have a platform," she said in a confident and upbeat tone.

I replied, "Oh, okay … let's share it!"

"It is our tagline—'facilitating the convergence of mind, body, and spirit'!" she said, beaming with excitement and as if she just correctly answered a trivia question on a prime-time game show.

I smiled and said, "Thank you!" and then looked at Suzanne and said, "I think this as a good place as any to discuss the difference between a tagline and a Brand Platform. What do you think?"

Suzanne rubbed her chin and replied, "I agree!" Moving to the second flip chart in the room she wrote a few words in bold caps—**External Expression and High Concept.**

"First," she started, "a tagline, unlike a Brand Platform, is an external phrase that expresses the tone of your brand to the market. It is designed to be catchy and memorable so that it stays in the mind of your customer, reinforcing a positive association with your brand. Second, it should set you apart from everyone else and describe what your focus is. It's like an advertising slogan or even in the case of marketing a movie in Hollywood, it is what is referred to as a 'high concept' or phrase used to convey what the movie is all about." Pointing to the words on the chart, Suzanne reinforced, "Kyla, again thank you for sharing this. Your tagline certainly has these critical elements."

"Can anyone think of examples of other brand taglines you know of?" I asked. The group threw out a few taglines:

Nike®—"Just Do It"

Wal-Mart®—"Save Money. Live Better."

Walgreens®—"The Pharmacy America Trusts"

"These are all great examples of taglines—external expressions of the brand—and are clearly designed to catch the attention of the consumer," I said.

Suzanne continued as she moved back to the first flip chart and a new sheet. She wrote the words "Internal Expression, Timeless Quality, and Essence" and said, "Conversely, a Brand Platform (or essence) is an *internal expression* of your brand. It is the heart and soul or essence of who you are as a brand. It is an internal expression that is inspiring and instinctively understood by employees yet is constant and enduring." She paused, allowing the group to soak it in, and then asked, "Does anyone know Starbucks' Brand Platform?" Again, another long pause as they were thinking.

Suzanne revealed, "It's 'Daily inspiration.' Notice that there is no mention of the products the company sells!"

"Oh of course; that makes total sense," said Stefan. "Their brand is very inspiring every time I visit. It is the experience of the coffee, the music, the buzz of the conversations in the place, the whole environment that is inspiring; it helps regulate my mood."

I added, "Very nurturing to the human spirit."

"How about Hallmark?" Suzanne continued. No one seemed to know. She revealed, "It's 'Caring Shared.'" There was a pause, and she then asked, "What about Ritz Carlton?"

"Oh, I know what theirs is," replied Sadie. "We are ladies and gentlemen serving ladies and gentlemen," and with a little smirk admitted, "I used to work for them."

"Ahh … and as you can see," continued Suzanne, "most of these Brand Platforms aren't readily known by those outside the business unless you've been an employee of one and are intimate with the internal workings and knowledge of the brand."

Meg interjected, "So it's about creating an internal perception of what the brand is all about so employees understand its underlying essence and how they need to behave and emulate that way of being?"

"Exactly," replied Suzanne. "Meg, you hit the nail on the head! Your Brand Platform is the overall essence of your brand, clearly defining internally its fundamental and enduring nature. It doesn't have to speak about the business you are in but rather the emotive nature of how the brand is expressed. It is the emotional connection the Brand Platform elicits in the mind of the employee and how that is transferred through behaviors that create an emotional connection for customers to the brand."

Everyone was nodding their heads. I could feel the cogwheels churning in their minds as I observed and smiled at the discussion unfolding.

Meg continued, "I can see the nuances in the differences now. Our tagline is a good one. It expresses what we do for our clients in simple yet clear terms, but it doesn't express the heart and soul of what we are all about, internally, as a brand, which gives meaning to what we do in our work day in and day out. So we have a bit of work to do on creating our Brand Platform!"

"Yes, and we'll do that shortly," I said. "Now let's discuss the concept of your brand's promise and do an exercise that combines the development of both the brand platform and brand promise, together."

Holding the remote to the DLP projector, I clicked from black screen to a normal full screen showing a colorful slide with the words "Your Brand's Promise." The description read: "This is the promise you commit to and follow through in every action, every interaction, every business activity, and every customer touch point. It is lived internally and externally through the company. It sets the rules for doing business. It drives budgets and stops arguments." I said, "I love this timeless description from Kristin Zhivago, respected marketing consultant and editor of the *Marketing Technology* newsletter, in the July/August 1994 issue. "To be successfully positioned, the Ecologé brand must promise differentiated benefits that are relevant and compelling to your market." On the screen popped up

*DIFFERENTIATED BENEFITS = WIIFM.* "Anyone know what WIIFM is?" I asked.

"What's in it for me!" answered Stefan.

"Exactly," replied Suzanne. "What's in it for the Ecologé customer? Why should they do business with you? What is it you provide better or different from every other Joe or Jane in your industry? Know this: your competitors can copy your 'hard stuff'—your price points, products and services, marketing gimmick, etc. What they cannot copy as easily is the 'soft stuff'—how you show up and deliver in distinctive ways to your customers; through systems and processes, your distinctive culture, and how you nurture them in all the behind-the-scenes activities that support the entire experience. These behind-the-scenes activities include how you train your staff and the sensory and behavioral aspects you create that evoke tremendous emotional bonding to your brand in the minds of your customers."

Ty asked, "So what differentiated benefits can Ecologé leverage that would make the brand more relevant and compelling to the market? I have to admit, there are a lot of brands capitalizing on the eco-friendly, natural, and organic body-care philosophy. I just searched the topic on the Internet the other day and found more 'Joe and Jane' Web sites than I could have possibly imagined."

Before either Suzanne or I could reply, Meg stepped in with, "You're absolutely right, Ty. There are a lot of them out there, way more than I ever imagined until we started our research." She pulled out a three-ring binder from her computer bag and placed it on the conference room table. "I've given my entire team copies of this material. Kyla has been doing lots of research. We know what our competitors claim, but I'm willing to bet they don't have an edge like we do because we dug deep into our Brand DNA these last two days."

"That's good. You're doing your homework. Now let's leverage this Brand DNA and get started on creating your Brand Platform and Promise," Suzanne instructed.

I turned and headed to the CD player to find the right music to allow the team's creative juices to flow. Meg and her team begin the creative process of fleshing out their unique Brand Platform and Promise.

**SEE PART II: READER EXERCISES, CHAPTER 3 EXERCISE, for your BRAND PLATFORM and PROMISE DEVELOPMENT and ECOLOGE's final outputs.**

# CONSULTANTS' CORNER

Many business owners believe that once they develop a tagline it serves as the differentiator and unique benefit they provide to their customers. The tagline is an important part of externally expressing the brand, but it is not in and of itself a differentiator, nor the internal propeller that drives differentiation. It is a take-away benefit the customer can expect. Your brand's promise reflects your brand's way of being and the association of your brand's message through consistent behavior in the mind of the customer. By clearly defining the four components of your Brand DNA (values, style, differentiators, and standards) and understanding why a Brand Platform and Promise are the final ingredients, you can then begin to more strategically position and create the optimal brand experience that:

- Focuses your efforts on creating *systems and processes* that enable and support the delivery of powerful sensory and behavioral experiences for your brand.
- Reflects a *culture* emulating the unique *values and style attributes and differentiators and standards* associated with your brand.
- Creates consistency that keeps your *customers coming back for more.*
- Demonstrates a strong point of view for *what* your brand *stands for.*
- Creates *true distinction* for your products and services.
- Makes your customers *fanatical about doing business with you.*
- Creates a sense of belief and *unequivocal trust* in your brand.
- *Reinforces the promise* you make through every customer touch point.
- Enlists your employees and customer as *brand champions.*

## Brand Platform

Your Brand Platform is the underlying but overall *essence of your brand* and what you stand for. It tells your employees exactly what your brand is all about and how they need to show up to reflect the brand daily. It doesn't refer to a particular product or service but to the "gestalt" of what the brand stands for. In *Brand Aid,* VanAuken refers to your brand essence as "constant, timeless and enduring. It will not change across geographies or in different situations."[1] It is action-oriented and highly expressive of what you stand for.

Hallmark's Brand Platform of "Caring Shared" references nothing about being in the greeting card industry; instead it hones in on the essence of the meaning behind the brand. It is timeless, enduring, and constant. Nike's Brand Platform is "authentic athletic performance." Disney's is "fun, family entertainment." It often reflects the most distinctive attributes of your brand's personality or style. It immediately engages employees. They instinctively know what it means. It energizes and inspires them. In a client example later in this section, you will see how this client's Brand Platform took off like wildfire in the organization with a few key yet compelling words.

## Brand Promise

Your brand's promise is a declaration that reflects a compelling and differentiating experience for your customers and sets the rules for doing business. In his books, *The BrandMindset® and The BrandPromise®* author Duane Knapp recommends that a brand promise be written to "define the key functional and emotional benefits from the customers' point of view after experiencing the product and service you provide."[2] Your brand's promise must balance the evolving nature and aspirational goals of your brand against what you are able to deliver to both your employees and customers. Your brand's promise needs to be a stretch yet be realistic in order to motivate and inspire action among your employees to follow through on it day in and day out.

Your brand's promise is not an advertising message to customers but rather an internal behavioral declaration that everyone in the organization must understand, embrace, and emulate as a way of being. Rest assured, your customers will understand it when you consistently deliver on it. This raises another compelling question. How do you balance the actions your employees strive to deliver with the reality of what they can deliver if they do their best?

There are five key actions every brand can take that if done well will allow you to bridge this gap and create a balance.

1.  Define and articulate your unique, authentic Brand DNA Platform and Promise as a team with your key employees. Communicate, communicate, communicate! Your employees

need to clearly understand your Brand DNA story and what the brand is all about. Get creative in the hiring and orientation process when you recruit employees. Make sure you hire the right employees that fit the values and style attributes of your brand. Ensure that your employees understand how your Brand DNA translates to the desired brand experience you want to create for them and your customers. Create on-the-job-training opportunities so employees can practice how to deliver the right brand experience. Get creative with how you communicate through different ways such as an internal newsletter, a company intranet, blog postings, employee orientation, and team meetings. Employees need to understand clearly what your brand is all about (through sight, sound, the environment, etc.) so they can show up in every way possible to express your brand with passion, integrity, and authenticity. As reported by Watson Wyatt Worldwide in a 2005/2006 Communication ROI Study, "Firms that communicate effectively are 4.5 times more likely to report high levels of employee engagement versus firms that communicate less effectively." [3]

2. Engage everyone to live and embody your brand's promise. When people are engaged, they are more inspired and energized. Engagement has to start from the top. Management is a critical role model. Management's thoughts, actions, and decisions have to demonstrate that you walk your talk. This shows consistency and integrity with management in living the brand.

3. Ensure that your employees know how their roles link to the goals of your brand. When employees understand how their roles link to the vision, values, and essence of your brand it creates the opportunity for them to support your brand and demonstrate their active commitment. Ask your employees to create a simple recognition program that everyone can participate in to build and reaffirm behaviors that support your brand.

4. Verify that your business processes support your brand's promise. Your processes should not get in the way of delivering your brand's promise but rather enable and facilitate its delivery consistently. If your brand emphasizes convenience

for your customers, then make sure your processes enable this convenience to be provided seamlessly through every aspect of your brand through your employees.

5.  Empower your employees to live up to your brand's promise. Empowered employees demonstrate a certain confidence and know how and when to break the rules while they use good judgment to deliver on your brand's promise.

Your Brand Platform and Promise should drive every employee's thoughts, actions, and customer interaction as well as the company's every decision. If you begin to waver or compromise, you begin to erode the credibility of your brand. Think about companies like Enron and Arthur Andersen. They both paid a hefty price for not adhering to their brand promises. Or consider, more recently, AIG. Where were the values in action behind these companies? What happened to the focus on their brand promises when decisions were made that went against the values that reflected what they stood for?

Companies that truly live their Brand Platform and Promise are persistent in their resolve to create cultural environments that are sustainable and behind the brand in every way. This is what we refer to as an authentic brand. These brands create enormous trust with their customers, employees, investors, Wall Street, and the government. That trust is built on their reputation, consistency, and distinctiveness, which in turn build an emotional bond with employees and customers.

## Client Example
We worked with a client in the tanning industry. This was a highly reputable, award-winning company that had led the market as an innovator in the industry and would accept nothing less. The market viewed the industry as a commodity. They were, nonetheless, determined to elevate the value proposition and growth of their brand in the minds of the market.

As part of a comprehensive brand assessment project, the Brand Ascension Group facilitated a Brand DNA session for this client. This encompassed a powerful brainstorming session with key leaders in the business to discover their unique Brand DNA: those qualities (differentiators, style, values, and standards) unique to them and to which no other competitor could lay claim. This facilitation resulted in the development of their own unique brand platform and brand's promise, which set the rules for doing business going forward.

**Their Brand Platform:**
*Excellence, Simply Mind-blowing Experience*

**Their Brand Promise:**
*The ultimate light therapy experience where unparalleled customer service combined with passion, confidence, and integrity creates a lasting impression!*

This set the stage for our client to begin the process of elevating the brand and to show up in every way to provide a "Simply Mind-blowing Experience" for all stakeholders—prospective and existing employees and customers. A crucial step involved the Brand Ascension Group's Branded for Hire[SM] process, a program tailored to dramatically increase the success rate in employee hiring and retention by identifying and hiring new people who share the values and style attributes of the brand. This process created a paradigm shift in the collective thinking and actions of the leadership team. The modeling of behaviors with existing employees made a huge impression as they were exposed also to this new way of being: "Simply Mind-blowing Experience." It started a buzz within the organization. Employees started speaking and emulating "Mind-blowing Experiences" to one another and to customers in unique and empowering ways. This client revamped their operational and training processes. Some examples include:

- Their employee handbook is all about "Simply Mind-blowing Experience" throughout every customer touch point.
- They've created a consistent look and feel with the retail store, their signage, paperwork, applications, business cards, etc.
- Thank-you cards are sent to new customers within two weeks with a $10 gift card.
- They have a calendar of events that lists their hours, a bulletin of packages/pricing, and different special incentives: ladies' night, guys' day, double-your-points day, etc.
- Employees remember guest names and use the name in the course of conversation several times.
- There is constant customer interaction throughout the store.
- They stay on top of what their customers like and their buying patterns.

- Their referral program rewards existing customers with a $25 gift certificate, and the referred customer gets fifty points to use toward tanning.

They experienced great results:

- Average transactions per customer are significantly higher ranging from 300 – 400 percent.
- Employee behaviors and attitudes are highly relevant to what the brand stands for.
- They have a procedure for everything that happens in the store.
- There are fewer employee issues, and higher expectations were achieved.
- The employee interview process has been enhanced to be congruent with the brand, so they are hiring better-quality people that fit their brand.
- They have decreased employee turnover, which has been a significant cost savings.

So what actions are you going to create to cause you to behave more congruent with what you say you are? What is the essence of your brand? What is that promise that you commit to live up to at every customer touch point? At every employee touch point? What will inspire and propel your employees?

# CHAPTER 4

## *Myth: Branding is Marketing*

*Marketing messages are so pervasive that
they are no longer persuasive!*
*—"Buzz" guru John Taylor,
president of Say So Marketing,
a word-of-mouth event-marketing
service in New York City*

## THE CHALLENGE ...

Two weeks have passed.

"Buzzz!" went my office intercom.

"Good morning, Suzanne. Meg is here for her 8:30 with you," my assistant Liz said.

"Great, Liz. Give me one minute and send her in. I'll notify Carol."

"Well hello, Meg. Carol is on her way in. You look great today!" I said.

"Thanks! I feel really good too. I took what we talked about in our last session to heart and dove into developing my brand's style. It was a great excuse to go clothes shopping and beef up my wardrobe!" Meg posed to show off her new attire.

"I'm impressed—you are a quick study!" I winked and smiled.

"I cannot tell you how long it has been since I bought a new suit! What was so cool about it is that I actually had a defined image in my mind of what my style was (see the chapter 2 brand style attributes selection)—chic, avant-garde, personable, and savvy—thanks to our previous Brand DNA session, and I found several outfits that more accurately represent me and my Ecologé brand. I gotta tell you, this is really starting to be fun!" Meg set down her purse and branding binder and took a seat on the overstuffed couch.

"Bet you never thought that the process of conscious, strategic branding could be so fun and creative!" I affirmed as I offered her a selection of assorted exotic teas.

Meg said, "I'm starting to build a whole new love affair with my business, believe it or not. I am definitely more conscious of all the things I have been doing to grow it—especially with my employees. I'm even noticing where the gaps are in terms of being congruent with our newly identified values and style attributes."

Meg sipped her white fusion apricot tea and continued, "Get this: on the heels of our Brand DNA session, I actively engaged my staff in owning and understanding our brand's values and style at our weekly meeting by talking about new behaviors they could invent to affirm our brand attributes. They were so enthusiastic about the DNA that their excitement and positive comments helped reaffirm that they wanted more direction or structure, or as you call it, a road map, that they could get their arms around. Their comments and expanded ideas on our new attributes blew me away and helped them become more conscious of their everyday activities on the job. It energized the whole meeting and took it in a powerful direction. So I am ecstatic with completing my first exercise! And ready to keep this brand discovery process rollin'!"

"Good morning everyone," announced Carol. She entered the room with her laptop under her left arm and a thermos of tea in her right hand. "My apologies for running late, I was on the phone with a client in Australia, finalizing some brand-diagnostic results. But I am eager to hear about your last two weeks and the outputs of your last exercise and how you will be implementing it into the Ecologé environment!"

Meg briefed Carol on our earlier conversation as I temporarily powered down my cell phone.

"Sounds like you're taking the right steps to consciously refine the Ecologé brand and are beginning to build a powerful brand road map. And it's great that you're including your staff in the creation and affirmation of it following the Brand DNA session. Now they have ownership and will be more willing and apt to follow through with truly living it! Great work!" praised Carol.

Meg beamed. "I have a question for you, though. One of the local cable company reps popped in the other day with a new value-added, bundled special they are running this month for electronic advertising and wanted us to take advantage of the cost savings. It sounds pretty good, but I wanted to get your take on the package."

I thought to myself, here we go again. Did she just not get our message completely? Now that we've finished the Brand DNA, she immediately wants to ramp up on marketing as the next step to build her business.

As Carol and I often experience with our clients, Meg and her team went immediately back on the marketing band wagon. Because of their new energy and excitement around the brand, they didn't realize that there was still a lot of internal work to be done prior to creating an effective, congruent message for the external campaign. This was typical and tempting, especially when media representatives package what is perceived to be a great deal.

"Oh, and ..." Meg added before either Carol or I could respond, "I am also running out of business cards for me and my staff and need to reorder soon and get my beautiful new logo design out there! And I thought about running another ad in three trade magazines, using our new logo identity to build on my brand recognition and to showcase a new product line. What do you think? I might go over my annual marketing budget (18 percent of revenue), but I think this time it will work!"

(See the Consultants' Corner for a full critique of the logo design compared to the newly invented Brand DNA of Ecologé.)

"Whooaa!" I said and threw my hands up in the air. "Take a deep breath, Meg. You are running a mile a minute because you are inspired by redefining your brand! That inspiration and motivation is so great to see! But there are many things we have yet to do to implement any action that you and your team have put on paper. Have you even taken another inquisitive review of your new logo design and matched or compared it with your DNA? There are several questions to be asked and confirmed before you move forward. We'll take some time to review your logo design against your new DNA. Your situation is typical of a common trap that a lot of business owners fall into when they have a new idea, new look, or inspiration about their business. They immediately want to get it on the air and out to their market."

Carol added quickly, "She's right; the danger in a hasty move like this, Meg, is that you have yet to fully implement and operationalize these ideas into your internal environment. Realistically, these attributes you developed for your values and style have not been fully incorporated into the Ecologé brand's way of being. We also need to guide you through several other complementary applications of your brand's DNA before Ecologé embarks on another marketing campaign."

"But won't I be missing out on this cost-saving opportunity to brand my business?" Meg questioned. "I thought that was the whole idea—to get the word out about my brand and be distinct from my competition?"

"You are only going to be missing out on throwing away precious marketing funds that cannot fix or increase your external business revenue when you haven't yet done the due diligence required by internal conscious branding strategies," I cautioned.

"As a matter of fact," Carol said, "think back to your Brand DNA session. Do you recall the differences between branding and marketing?" Carol moved to the flip chart and illustrated with colored markers the words "Marketing Is the Process Of" in an attempt to jog Meg's memory.

"Oh, yes! Now I remember! Isn't it about the different ways we use to communicate our message? Like press releases, direct mail, and radio and TV campaigns?" Meg recalled.

"Exactly," I said. "Let's revisit this concept, because it's important that you and your team keep this in the forefront of your minds. It's easy to slip back into a behavior or way of thinking that you are accustomed to until you replace that behavior permanently with a new one by practicing it. We are all guilty of this! But it is your continued inspiration and inquisitiveness that keeps you and other successful brand leaders on the cutting edge!" I emphasized.

I stood up and reached for several other colored markers sitting on the coffee table and walked toward Carol and the prepared flip chart. "Let's continue and remind ourselves of the key differences between the function of marketing and the process of branding; then we'll create some scenarios to help you internalize the distinctions. Remember that branding is the process of defining and living the core message you want your customers, employees, and vendors to perceive. So when we brand an organization we dig deep to define its core attributes and then set up actions and behaviors that enable and support it to live that message throughout every facet of the organization. These actions can include many things from answering the phone to an initial face-to-face client meeting, actual service delivery experience, follow-up and invoicing the client, and much more.

"Now we'll provide you and your team with an exercise to help you operationalize what you've learned. We cannot forget all the internal work you did on creating Ecologé's unique DNA; we must always reflect back on that DNA so we can assure that the brand is showing up as you intended, which is part of the process of brand management is. Sound good?" I smiled and waited for an acknowledgement from Meg.

Meg repositioned herself in the overstuffed couch, grabbed her binder and Ecologé pen, and said, "With all the years I've had in my corporate position, I am continually amazed at what I don't know when it comes to branding! I'm excited and I'll admit a little impatient, so let's get going!"

**SEE PART II: READER EXERCISES, CHAPTER 4 EXERCISE, for your REASSESS YOUR MARKETING MESSAGE exercise and ECOLOGE's final outputs.**

# CONSULTANTS' CORNER

More often than not we (BA Group) find ourselves coaching our clients to hold off on any additional marketing expenditures or allocations until we can get them implementing some of the internal Brand DNA road map they have developed through our consultative Brand DNA processes. Their natural reaction is resistance, because for all of their business life they have been told that marketing is a necessity and the foundation for building and sustaining a business.

We hear the same debate, "How can I build my business without letting people know who I am and what I sell?" Unfortunately, many businesses have been misled by that philosophy and get caught in a spiral of spending on a variety of marketing mediums with little to show for their investment. We see them reach out to a market that is too broad and untargeted, a market that may not truly understand the value of the message, or a market that cannot afford the product or service advertised, among other issues. But the real dilemma and waste of marketing dollars occurs in two key ways: 1) no real differentiating, consistent customer experience; and 2) lack of the development and implementation of powerful measurement tools to assess the efforts, tweak, and reconfigure for stronger outputs.

Meg was experiencing the same habitual reaction—*spend money on marketing and my business will grow!* Again, this is a natural, almost knee-jerk reaction that is based on past learning or even what an entrepreneur believes is logical. Take a moment to truly understand the function of marketing and how it differs, but complements, the function of branding. The Brand Ascension Group's definition of each is as follows:

Marketing = the process of *communicating* and *spreading* your *message.* (External)

Branding = the process of *defining the core perception of* and *actioning* (through behaviors, systems and processes, and environment) your *message*. (Internal)

Read these definitions again and again and again. Internalize them. You will begin to discern the huge difference between the two functions. Now think about this: how can you effectively communicate or disseminate your brand's message if you haven't yet spent the time and done the due diligence to create and live your brand's message?

Remember to refer back to your completed DNA often, your road map, to remind yourself how you express your brand through your internal actions and behaviors and ensure that they are congruent with your external advertising messages. We know that Meg's work on the Ecologé Brand DNA exposed several distinct style attributes—namely, chic, avant-garde, personable, and savvy. How, then, should these attributes play a role or influence her way of marketing (dissemination and communication of the message)? Where she places ads, how they are graphically represented, and what specific brand vocabulary used are all decisions that will now be based on her DNA road map. These specific details must be considered when disseminating the message and must be congruent with those DNA attributes attached to Ecologé. This is how the brand begins to take on and embody the three most powerful characteristics of a successful brand: consistency, distinctiveness, and relevancy (which will be discussed in greater detail in the upcoming chapters). With the onset of new forms of exposure, such as social media (LinkedIn, Twitter, Plaxo, Facebook, MySpace, and countless others), it is more important than ever to differentiate your brand with specific detail to include your unique brand values, style (company personality), and differentiators in your approach through these mediums.

As you can guess, if you spend money on marketing a message before you create, and most importantly, live and embody the message at the internal level of the business, the customer's trust will never be affirmed when the external message says one thing and the internal behavior of the company says another. This common situation often causes confusion at the subconscious level of your customers and will lead them to seek products and services elsewhere as they look for a vendor who provides that level of consistency and assurance for their expectations.

How do we know that being highly conscious and paying close attention to the creation of your brand's desired perception it wants to own and then living it works? Take Starbucks as an example. (We chose this highly successful brand because of its current, proven, business branding model and its ability to adapt and innovate in any economy or circumstance.) In the first twelve years of Starbuck's growth, the company spent an average of less than one percent of its annual revenues on the function of marketing.[1] This begs the question—then how did Starbucks grow to several billion dollars in revenue as of this writing?

Many marketing experts theorize that a whopping 8–12 percent of total revenue should be dedicated to expenses tied to a strategic marketing plan. So how did Starbucks do it, against the traditional rules of building a business?

It's quite simple: Starbucks puts much effort toward creating and living the brand's message through actions and behaviors. By concentrating on its internal infrastructure (e.g., its people/culture, systems and processes, leadership, and mission/vision), they "poured" a powerful foundation that launched it into the people business, not the coffee business! Starbucks set out to create the "third place" for patrons to frequent, aside from their offices and homes. Their mission statement says it all: *To inspire and nurture the human spirit—one person, one cup, and one neighborhood at a time.* Need we say more?

Another great example is Marriott Hotels. Believe it or not, they started out as a root-beer stand! Now the company is a market leader in the hospitality industry. How did it get there? By turning a lot of its focus inward—to its own culture, values, and what its brand stands for. One of its core ideologies when hiring new talent is "taking care of the associates," because management believes that satisfied and engaged employees will take care of the customers. Marriott takes the time to select its employees and, once they have been hired, provide them with training opportunities to keep them motivated and engaged. The company actively invests in training. It also requires that its franchisees and property owners do the same. The care and attention to whom it hires and how it trains helps it ensure its ability to satisfy its guests.

This is a perfect time to further discuss the differences between your *external* and *internal* business activities and what is included at both levels. (Figure 3.1, The Brand Tree, provides an illustration of this distinction.) Most of us understand the external levels of branding through the function of marketing; this level incorporates all the activities we use to disseminate the brand message into our targeted marketplace, like developing our name, the advertising, the look and feel of our corporate identity, what products and services we offer, public relations, our external signage, etc. Collectively, all these things are critical in the creation of consistency with our intended brand experience.

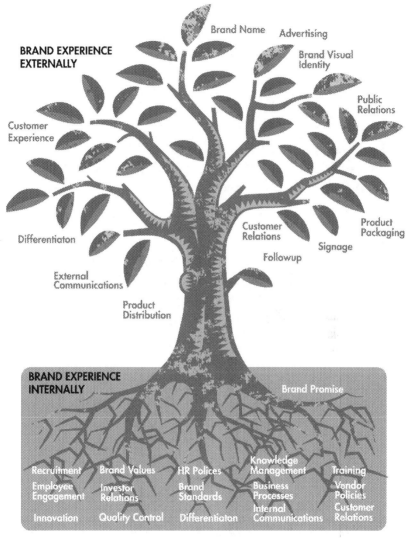

Figure 3.1

But none of these external activities will create a powerful, distinctive brand experience separate from the internal brand strategies that are put in place. Internal branding encompasses the organization's brand values, internal communications, customer relations, training, staff motivation, systems and processes, leadership, culture, etc.

Start seeing yourself as a key player in assisting your employees in their efforts to live your brand and create the culture that resonates and affirms the brand experience (internally) first and then to the customers' experiences (externally).

Once the internal brand strategies are in place and a foundation of the organization, then the external branding/marketing efforts begin to have meaning for the customer. The symbols, advertising, and environments then create assimilation and congruency at an emotional level in the mind of your market—a powerful and high-impact mechanism that leverages their experience with you, your products, and your services.

When Meg began to turn her focus more internally to her employee team rather than externally (marketing), she was able to create the infrastructure that supports the external message. This strategy helps reaffirm the trust in the customer's mind through Ecologé's efforts in showing up as consistent, relevant, and distinctive. The Ecologé brand began to blossom with every area of focus Meg put forth internally. Again, we have continually reminded Meg to refer back to her DNA—these are the core attributes of the Ecologé brand. Staying true to its DNA will streamline and simplify the process of growing the brand. The Ecologé DNA acts as "checks and balances" in how you operationalize and evolve the brand within the various facets of the business.

Now let's dissect Ecologé's new logo design and test it against Meg's Brand DNA. (See figure 3.2.)

Figure 3.2

*These are the questions that serve as the basis for analysis:*

1. Does the logo represent the *style* attributes of Ecologé (chic, avant-garde, personable, and savvy)? In our opinion, the overall logo is a bit heavily weighted. Yes, the accent mark helps with the argument for it being chic but does not truly represent

"savvy." The aesthetics don't convey a sense of knowledge or astuteness. The colors are dark and muted but come close to representing colors in our natural environment. This look may get lost on the shelves of boutiques and not energize or intrigue the customer to explore.

2. Does the logo represent the *values* of Ecologé? *(environmentally-conscious, harmony, purity, simplicity)*? Overall the logo is simple, but the current choice of fonts creates a bulky, clunky feel, not *simplistic*, light, and *pure*. Although not all corporate identity systems need graphic symbols, the absence of one on this logo misses a potentially powerful opportunity to evoke additional emotions from the customer reflecting *harmony, environmentally conscious,* and *personable*). 83 percent of everything humans remember is obtained visually.[2] This research justifies the case for the use of an icon in conjunction with an appropriate font for the name of the company.

## Let's Talk Briefly about the Psychological Effects of Color

While perceptions of color are somewhat subjective, there are some color effects that have universal meaning. Colors in the red area of the spectrum are known as *warm colors* and include red, orange, and yellow. These warm colors evoke emotions ranging from feelings of warmth and comfort to feelings of anger and hostility.

Colors on the blue side of the spectrum are known as *cool colors* and include blue, purple, and green. These colors are often described as calm but can also call to mind feelings of sadness or indifference.

What are you trying to express with your brand's corporate identity colors? How do you support that within your business environment and the customer experience?

We chose to update Meg's current logo with a particular shade of green and blue for these attributes:

## The Color Psychology of Green[3]

Green is a cool color that symbolizes nature and the natural world. Green also represents tranquility, good luck, and health.

- Researchers have also found that green can improve reading ability. Some students may find that laying a transparent sheet of green paper over reading material increases reading speed and comprehension.
- Green is often used in decorating for its calming effect. For example, guests waiting to appear on television programs often wait in a "green room" to relax.
- Green is thought to relieve stress and help healing. Those who have a green work environment experience fewer stomachaches.
- Consider how green is used in language: green thumb, green with envy, greenhorn.

## The Color Psychology of Blue[4]

Blue calls to mind feelings of calmness or serenity. It is often described as peaceful, tranquil, secure, and orderly.

- Blue is often used to decorate offices because research has shown that people are more productive in blue rooms.
- Blue can also lower the pulse rate and body temperature.

## Samples of Heavy Fonts

| | |
|---|---|
| **IMPACT** | **ARIAL BLACK** |
| **BAUHAUS 93** | **BODONI MT BLACK** |
| **FRANKLIN GOTHIC HEAVY** | **Old English Text** |

## Samples of Light Fonts

| | |
|---|---|
| FUTURA LIGHT | CENTURY GOTHIC |
| **ALBERTUS MEDIUM** | BATANG |
| GIL SANS | GARAMOND |

We believe that it is worth exploring a few more alternatives in the design of the logo to better represent and reflect the Brand DNA. Remember that your logo is not the brand but is a distinctive, congruent representative symbol that remains consistent in all applications and reaffirms your brand's promise experience.

We cannot discuss the logo image attributes without mentioning the importance of the final application of the image onto paper. Your stationery, business cards, brochures, etc., will all need to be printed on paper. There are thousands of different paper stocks. Make sure your designer understands your Brand DNA so that he or she can recommend appropriate paper samples to choose from (choices include high gloss, matte, and dull finishes, plus textures like linen, laid, antique, columns, etc.). For example, Ecologé will begin to review recycled paper stock samples so it can also include the universal "recycled" symbol on its collateral pieces. The choice to include this symbol is powerful to those it serves as well as completely congruent with its environmentally conscious brand value. Ecologé shows up as "practicing what it preaches," which is a powerful trust generator.

Why use recycled paper? (http://www.treecycle.com/info.html)

*Reduce Energy Consumption*
• 60–70 percent energy savings over virgin pulp.
• The paper industry is the third largest user of energy in the United States.

*Protect Natural Resources*
• The United States uses one hundred million tons of paper a year, and usage is increasing.
• Recycled paper uses 55 percent less water and helps preserve our forests.
• Recycling of waste paper creates more jobs.

*Reduce Pollution*
• The paper industry is one of the largest water polluters in the world.
• Recycled paper reduces water pollution by 35 percent and air pollution by 74 percent and eliminates many toxic pollutants.

After our collaborative review and creative critique with Meg on this latest upgraded design, she asked for our help in further developing a more congruent look and feel for her final corporate identity. We were honored by the request and immediately began discussing how we could incorporate her Brand DNA into a pure, harmonious, simplistic, and chic design.

One week later …

After a week of review with the Brand Ascension Group and our creation of several, suitable design schematics and tagline developments representing the Ecologé brand, Meg was delighted to make a final decision and unveiled logo design winner (Figure 3.3) to her staff. She heard a roaring round of applause!

Figure 3.3

As you can see, we developed a powerful, concise tagline, thanks to the road map provided by their brand DNA. This tagline gets to the core of the "WIIFM" (What's In It For Me) for the customer. The customers of Ecologé are highly sensitive to issues regarding the environment—from what is put in and on their bodies to what "footprint" is left on the earth in terms of waste.

The stylized image of a body with the central sphere in the icon represents the core of the human element and human-kind's relationship with nature. Zooming out from the view of the body, you see the shape of a stylized eye, which represents inner wisdom and knowledge (savvy) of the power of nature and man's connection to it. And again, the blue and green hues were chosen for their healing and calming attributes.

So before we get into the usage of this new look and feel, remember that a *logo* is not the brand but rather the *symbol* that represents the brand. And remember that a brand is a perception that comes from a direct experience (with the business brand) or an indirect experience (e.g., referral from a friend). So when consumers make a purchase decision, they are buying the experience the brand provides them. When there is no distinction among experiences of one or more competing brands, then there is no real loyalty to any one of the brands. That is when a brand becomes a commodity in the mind of its market. For example, the element of convenience or price might play a bigger role in the purchase decision of a buyer at any given time (e.g., Wal-Mart is a brand perceived to be lower in prices than its closest competitor, Target).

So whether or not the logo is highly relevant with a look and feel representing the brand's attributes, the real test is in the experience the consumer perceives of the brand. However, when the logo and brand experience are in congruence with one another, the effect is exponential in affirming what the brand stands for through and through. Your customers will begin connecting the look and feel of your logo symbol to the actual experience they have with the brand.

But before you begin or continue to externally communicate your message, you need to begin or continue the process of creating it and then develop the standards of your brand's behavior (systems/processes, culture, etc.) and assure they are congruent.

Here's a great example:

Remember back in the summer of 2005 when General Motors was the first to launch a powerful TV and print campaign to its external market that promised employee discount pricing on every new car available to the average buyer? It was a powerful idea and great campaign. Unfortunately, within a matter of two weeks or so at least three other car manufacturers began touting the same message! What happened to GM's competitive advantage? Think of all the money it paid its high-end advertising firm to come up with that idea and implement it. We understand that copying is the best form of flattery, but when it costs you hundreds of thousands of dollars, it just doesn't sit that well! How do you compete with that?

When we talk about your, or Meg's, competitive advantage, we focus on the company's "soft stuff." We refer to your internal behaviors, systems and processes, and culture. This forces you to take a hard, comprehensive look into how the products and services are delivered to your customer. What is your customer's total experience? That's where your competitive advantage will be identified and leveraged. Think of this as opposed to focusing on the "hard stuff" like the pricing structure, the packaging, and the call to action, bundling product packages, and others.

Terry Bacon and David Pugh, authors of *Winning Behavior: What the Smartest, Most Successful Companies Do Differently*, noted that best-in-class companies had more than great products and services, a unique business model, and a wealth of talented employees; they also "out-behaved" their rivals and created behavioral advantages for themselves in the markets they served.[5] "Out-behaving" means they were significantly better than the norm in their industry.

Your distinctive behavioral attributes are the secret to powerful conscious branding strategies that are primarily "soft-dollar" and time investments. Until you have these or similar behaviors engrained into your infrastructure and embedded into the minds of your employees (every single one of them), any marketing dollars you spend to bring your customers to your "storefront" will be wasted, as the behaviors to instill the trust and create a "Wow" experience will be negligible.

Now, taking all the internal DNA work we have done so far with Meg and Ecologé to heart, we have created an alternate ad layout as a template so that all of Ecologé ads will begin to appear consistent and take on a repetitious, recognizable look and feel. Within seconds, Meg's customers will recognize an Ecologé ad and be drawn to it. We have expressed her internal DNA attributes in a visual way—very deliberately and strategically. The key is to remain consistent so that its customers will begin to form a trust in and loyalty to the brand.

### Ecologé's Ad Comparison …

Old Ad Layout: Figure 4.1               New Ad Layout: Figure 4.2

As you can see, there are definite differences in the old (Figure 4.1) and the new (Figure 4.2) ad layouts. The old layout is basic, sort of stodgy in its square format, and not nearly as inviting or embracing as the new ad. The old ad incorporates some harsh colors: scarlet red, yellow, green, and a dusty blue with a heavy stylized font that would be more appropriate for the tech industry.

The new layout exudes a softer feel, a more humanistic and personable, chic, and avant-garde style, and a look with colors that are invigorating.

It features an exotic-looking flower, a photo of product as a visual, and soft, rounded edges. The font is specifically chosen for its simplicity (sans serif Futura) and open, rounded feel—no frills, very clean and crisp. The layout also suggests a contemporary feel with the URL running up the side and the soft gradient of green to blue from left to right. The message includes Ecologé's Brand Platform mantra: simple, harmonious, evolving, which gives readers a sense of the company's approach to the products it produces and sells. There is also a sense of the company's philosophy and a perception of high quality because of the professional design of the ad. The logo icon is also used as a graphic element, ghosted in the background for a subliminal reaffirmation of the brand's visual symbol.

We continue to work with Meg to create more distinctive and compelling behaviors that reflect Ecologé's Promise and Platform as well as its overarching standards, values, and style. By doing this, Ecologé will serve its clients with congruency in its external marketing messages. As a result of the last portion of this exercise, we helped Ecologé implement a process for one of its touch points—incoming phone orders or customer questions. We advised Meg to create a partnership with a small boutique call center to better manage the incoming volume of calls. For example, when customers call Ecologé's toll-free line, they are immediately connected to this specially trained call center and a live person! This reflects its "personable" brand DNA style attribute.

The representatives from the call center and Meg's team are carefully trained to converse in a specific soothing, personable (Brand DNA style), assuring voice that is never raised. The customer is always asked a "well-being" question such as: "How are you *being* today?" There is light, instrumental music playing in the background and during a call transfer. When a caller is asked if he or she can be put on hold and the response is positive, they are introduced to a well-written Ecologé Magic Story narrated by an elegant and harmonious (Brand DNA value) female voice. This story educates the client on all the powerful details of specific differentiators of Ecologé, how the products are made, and the promise to the customer. This phone experience is specifically designed to be streamlined and integrated. Each Ecologé team member is empowered to make any necessary decisions to create the right experience for the client, on the fly and without question. After the call, phone operators are then requested to briefly identify the decision made on behalf of the client and the situation. This is kept in a database and reviewed/brainstormed with the team every week to help further elevate the customer experience if the same situation were to happen again.

You invent processes like this quickly with your own team using your key brand value and/or style attributes. Choose one of your unique style attributes and then choose a customer or an employee touch point within your business. Begin brainstorming how you can inculcate this attribute in the current process/behavior and see what manifests from your discussions! It is a great step toward becoming more and more brand conscious in your business.

# CHAPTER 5

## *Myth: My Customers Just Want the Best Price*

*In an emotional economy, success is judged
by a profound and indelible connection with
people through sensory experiences.*
                                        —*Marc Gobé,*
*Chairman and CEO of Desgrippes Globe New York,*
*"Why Advertisers Still Don't Get It,"*
*February 16, 2007, BusinessWeek.com*

## THE CHALLENGE

"Good afternoon, Meg," I said into my cell phone as I shut my car door. "Are we still on for our 2:00 PM? I'm on my way back to the office now to prepare."

"Sorry I hadn't called you back to confirm," Meg said, a bit flustered. "But I have been on the phone it seems like for hours, basically in a bidding war with a customer on a twelve-month contract on our latest product. Apparently they've been solicited by my competition and they're asking for comparable pricing, which means I have to cut my price by 18 percent to keep the contract! But, yes, we are still on today at 2:00 pm. I want to get your advice on how to manage this one!" she said with a sigh.

"Ahh, that's a classic!" I said as I instantly recognized the challenge. "This will be fun. I look forward to seeing you in a couple of hours ... but for now, take a deep breath, take five minutes, and breathe in some of your own relaxing lavender essential oils!"

"Okay, but I'm a bit concerned. They're a new client and are currently looking at our Dead Sea salt product line. I know ours is the best and most distinctive on the market. We go to a lot of effort to get real Dead Sea salts, not just salt. And there's the potential to sell the entire line. But right now the problem is much narrower. All they are concerned about is price!" Meg reiterated.

"Interesting. I want you to bring along everything that the customer has seen about this product. And then we'll strategize this one together!" I said.

"I knew I could count on the Brand Ascension Group to help! Thanks, and I'll see you soon!"

At 1:57 pm, Meg arrived at our offices with a computer briefcase and a tote bag of products in tow. We said our hellos and settled into our comfortable consulting area. Carol started in, "Suzanne briefed me on your earlier conversation regarding the bidding war with your customer. How did you leave the conversation with them?"

"Well," Meg said, releasing a big sigh, "I told them to give me twenty-four hours to consider it and/or restructure the contract. That's all I could think of to buy me some more time. This seems to be happening more and more, and I'm not sure how to handle it," Meg said with submission.

"I can imagine your frustration," Carol acknowledged, "but this is a great opportunity to state your case and truly begin to educate your retail client of your distinctions. It may even be an opportunity to find another customer—one who truly appreciates the value of your product line. But first, let's take a look at your latest product samples."

Meg, suddenly reenergized, got up from the couch and walked over to the table. She placed the tote bag gently on the table and began sifting through it. She pulled out three different sizes and packages for a detoxifying product made with perfectly blended genuine Dead Sea salt crystals.

"Do you know the power of the Dead Sea salts? Its mineral composition improves cell metabolism and contributes to restoration and regeneration. It also acts as a disinfectant of sorts and can help in removing harmful substances from the skin," Meg said as she slowly walked toward us, still thinking and strategizing in her own mind how to solve this issue.

Meg handed me one of the packages, and I began to read the descriptor on the packaging.

### Experience Dead Sea Salt Bathing:

*The beneficial effects of the Dead Sea salts on the skin and their unique therapeutic and beautifying powers have been recognized since ancient times. Cleopatra, considered the most beautiful woman in the world during her era, went to great expense and effort to obtain exclusive rights over the Dead Sea area. At her command, pharmaceutical and cosmetic factories were built near the Dead Sea. Their remains can still be seen today at Ein Bokek and Ein Gedi.*

*The use of Dead Sea bath salts is a soothing and experiential way to relax and absorb the powerful healing minerals of the Dead Sea. Scientifically proven with much research, the amazing efficacy of Dead Sea salts in alleviating skin diseases such as psoriasis and others has led thousands to experience relief. The salts are highly beneficial for minimizing muscle tension or for simply relaxing and enjoying a rejuvenating experience.*

*There's nothing like a soak in a Dead Sea salt bath. This practice was once relegated to high-end spas and expensive skin clinics, but now therapeutic salt baths are becoming a common, affordable practice in the privacy of our own homes.*

*A warm sea salt bath provides a vehicle for soothing, deep relaxation as well as a delicacy of minerals the skin relishes as they are absorbed.*

---

"What a great product for the stresses of our day and age. This text is a perfect composition of copy that would serve well as a separate hang tag too," I commented. Right away, I noticed the packaging. It was very different than the other Ecologé products we had seen. So my first question was "Why the different packaging?"

"Well, this product idea was conceived about nine months ago when I began doing some research on the Dead Sea after watching a documentary on TV. I threw the idea out to my current graphic designer to come up with several different layout designs that we thought represented the exotic area, and we chose this one because it was so unique—we thought it would stand out more," Meg touted. "Oh, I brought a sample of our competitor's line too so you can see who is also bidding on the account. These guys are cheaper, but they also include extra, unnecessary ingredients that can cause allergic reactions in some people."

Carol immediately said, "It absolutely is different, but here is the reason for the question. How will your loyal customers know, within seconds, that this is a product from their trusted Ecologé line? It's so unique that it doesn't even reflect YOUR brand's new look and feel, which is one of the first identifiers—sight—that creates an emotional bond."

I added, picking up two of the three sizes, "So in your efforts to be more distinctive in design, you may end up confusing your loyal market. They may not extend the trust to this line as they would if, visually, it represented the Ecologé look they have *learned* to trust. Your logo is not even that readily recognizable, and the color scheme of the package doesn't resemble any other color scheme in your other lines. Does that make sense?"

Meg pondered the statements from Carol and me and sat back in her seat. "Wow, why does this seem like the most obvious thing in the world to me now? I cannot believe I didn't think about this. I just handed the project off to my designer, along with a recording of that program I told you about a moment ago. She ran with it. I wasn't thinking in those terms, and neither was my designer."

I quickly explained our learning point, "When you change your packaging in ways that are not in harmony with your brand's known look and feel, it's like introducing a whole new brand to the marketplace instead of riding on the equity or history of your current product lines."

Carol added as she turned on the digital light projector and pointed to the drop-down screen, "And here's another important point, Meg." The following slide popped up on the screen.

## 99 Percent of Your Customers' Purchases Are Based on Emotion, Not Price!

"So Carol and Suzanne, how does changing my packaging change the 18 percent discount my customer wants?"

"Oh, yes. You mentioned having to play a bidding game with your customer, again, because of a competitor who is offering a lower-cost product. Our objective today is to get you beyond the thought that your customers just want the best price. The danger is that if you begin playing that game, you'll be forced, due to the cost of doing business, to slowly reduce the quality of products, services, and attention to your clients and be lumped in the commodity category of skin-care products. That's a spiral a lot of businesses at your growth stage fall victim to. But not with us," I said.

Carol quickly added, "That's why we're here. We are going to help you better define distinctions and value-added benefits of Ecologé, once again to your Brand's DNA differentiators and standards. These will come from service behaviors that PROVE to your customer that the Ecologé line of products is well worth the price as well as the product features."

"Exactly," I confirmed. "Think of it as your "Magic Story" of sorts. Based on your DNA, it is the story that expresses Ecologé's products and service-delivery philosophy in a way that is enduring, compelling, and congruent with your actual behaviors in how you do business. It is one of Ecologé's emotional components or links to the customers' mind's eye and overall perception of what they are buying and who they are buying from. Studies show that the more a customer is educated or aware of the company's philosophy, direction, contribution, and ideals/values, the more *relationship bonding* occurs," I said with passion.

I continued, "We would be remiss not to mention a profound statement made by Joseph Pine and James Gilmore in *The Experience Economy* that gets right at the core of our learning point. It states:

In the absence of a DISTINCTIVE brand experience,
PRICE becomes the DEFAULT in your customer's
PURCHASE decision. [1]

"What a true statement! Now, put your *consumer* shoes on and see how this resonates with making a *decision on how you choose* to spend your hard-earned money on products and services with specific brands. It is a solid bet that those choices are based on the memories or expectations of the actual experiences you've received or expect to receive from the brand."

Then I remembered another quick story to make my point. "Have you ever gone on a tour of a brewery or a winery?"

Meg replied, "Actually, no. I never have."

Carol said, "I hadn't either until we worked with a boutique winery that needed some help branding their limited line of blended wines. At our first meeting, the first thing we did was to take a tour of the forty-seven-acre vineyard. I was expecting this to take about one hour or so. It was so fascinating, and so much care was taken to transfer the details of the process, that we ended up taking three and a half hours! The tour was geared to the novice, wanna-be wine connoisseur and to fully demonstrate the process the winery goes through to produce the product. But I have to mention that more fascinating than the tour was our guide, Mr. Braven.

His passion, intensity, and commitment to perfection with his wine blends was absolutely commendable! After the tour, I was ready to be on his payroll and work at the winery!

"We were completely surprised, being wine enthusiasts, of the detail of art, intuition, and skill level it took to carefully craft some special quality ingredients in a secret recipe to produce this specific brand of blended wines.

"Fascinating and emotional! We developed a whole new depth and appreciation for the brand we were now consulting. The tour was priceless in providing us the information to move the brand forward in helping them define, create, and build it.

"We then asked Mr. Braven, 'Why doesn't your market know what you do at this detailed level?'

"Mr. Braven, who now insisted that we call him 'Ian,' said 'Well, I guess I thought they were just interested in the end product. The final flavor, aroma, nose, and color of the wine blends, not the process.'"

I continued, "That was the birthing of a new campaign of bringing the customer/user inward and behind the scenes to become educated as to the art of creating the product. The campaign literally took his market inside the wine master's world. We recommended they film their process—with bios, testimonials, and an excerpt on 'a day in the life' of the brand's loyal, skilled, and dedicated employees. This created an extraordinarily powerful "Magic Story" for the brand."

"They even had a pair of vineyard dogs that participated in the everyday winemaking events. Their beloved dogs are also now featured on the wine labels, including stories of how the dogs helped in the making of each specific blend, from guarding the wine barrels to chasing away rodents in the vineyards. Overall, the brand became much more experiential to their market. This provided an expanded emotional connection to the product. Within eight months of the new campaign, they started an exclusive VIP monthly wine club, too. This was huge for the brand and catapulted its growth over the next six months."

"Incredible, I get it," Meg replied, slowly and steadily. "I want to educate my customer base, but I didn't think they cared about the process. I didn't think it would matter that we brought those salts all the way from halfway around the world versus some other salt-processing place somewhere else in the world. I have been dying to tell them the details!"

"Your 'Magic Story,' Meg, will share your passion, philosophy, and motivation for your brand and what you are doing for your customers,"

Carol added. "It will also educate them on the quality processes; the means that Ecologé takes to compose 100 percent organic, natural products that 'enhance personal harmony through sensory activation of the mind, body, and spirit (brand promise),'" Carol finished with a wink to Meg.

I added, "With each purchase opportunity there are a myriad of decisions that your customers go through before they make the final move to buy or not. As Carol mentioned, the mind, body, and spirit aspects of the process are key to keep in your consciousness when launching new products that need to be congruent with your Brand DNA. For example, you've identified two of your values as purity and simplicity. How can you create a buying experience around these two values? We might suggest making it 'simple' for your customer to try the 'purity' of your Dead Sea salts product by bundling a sample size to another one or two of your products. This will give them a chance to experience the value of the product and want to come back for more."

Meg said, "Ahhh, that makes sense, but can you articulate a bit more on the mind, body, spirit decision processes?"

"Sure," I responded. "I'll start by reminding us that we are human beings and the only way we experience something is through our sensory receptors—sight, sound, taste, touch, smell, and intuition. With our senses come vibrations or energy, and with each vibration we individually associate an emotion or feeling.

"So," I continued, "based on our own life experiences, we assign different varying degrees of emotion to what we see, taste, hear, smell, feel, and intuit. And then there is that gestalt, or the feeling that the whole experience is greater than the sum of the individual parts, that is also taken in and processed and that provides us with our final buying decision. Our *mind* is our analytical self weighing all the logical and illogical scenarios when a buying opportunity presents itself. Our *body* provides us with the anticipated or real feelings that are a result of the sensory intakes within the situation. Our *spirit* is our sense of well-being and benefits, or not, when those vibrations manifest in the buying decision."

"Okay," Meg responded, "so let me see if I understand this fully. Take my Dead Sea salts product line and begin thinking through the buying decision based on the mind, body, spirit aspects of my customers' buying process. The mind will tell my customer whether the product is worth the price or perceived as a good value, among other analytical things. The customer's body feels the resulting emotions associated with the intake of her senses, like if this product smells right, looks right, has good packaging, feels right, sounds right, etc. And the customer's 'spirit' is like the overall final decision maker. That spirit compiles all of these mini-variables. Hmm, that gives me a whole new perspective in creating powerful differentiators and assuring that the product is congruent with my brand," she finished.

"I believe you're catching on here," Carol said in an assuring way. "You are actively involved in the research related to your products, aren't you?" she asked.

Meg continued, "Why, yes. I first became aware of a highly reputable research company from an article that I read regarding the little-known secret of natural products. I was astounded at the results! The article compared natural products to not-so-naturally created products, like the competition uses. I contacted this research company and have created an excellent relationship with them. In fact, they are researching and writing an article right now that compares specific products, including mine. They've already told me that to their knowledge nobody else is producing a product anywhere near the quality of ours.

"In addition, we have employed biologists, botanists, and dermatologists to compound the recipes of our organic products. These experts understand the fact that we are focused on becoming the eco-thought-leaders of our industry! Yes, yes ... I see where this is going!" Meg said.

"Today," I added with excitement, "we are also going to take a look at your customer touch points. Touch points are all the incidences where Ecologé touches its clients, covering all sorts of areas from phone contacts to Web exposure to direct mail, even invoicing or e-mail responses. These touch points can greatly add or take away from the customer's experience with the product. So this topic is powerful when we talk about customers shopping for value versus price."

"Once we do the due diligence to dissect these areas," Carol added, "we will be able to better adapt your current behavioral protocols to your recently invented Brand DNA and make sure those touch points are showing up perceptively congruent with what you want your brand to be."

Meg readjusted and sat closer to the edge of her seat. "Right; build it and they will come!" she affirmed with a smile.

"You got it," said Carol. "We've got some work to do today; let's get started!"

**SEE PART II: READER EXERCISES, CHAPTER 5 EXERCISE, for your MAGIC STORY development exercise and ECOLOGE's final outputs.**

# CONSULTANTS' CORNER

Meg's situation is common in the small-business arena. It is easy to become a victim of price wars. Our advice—if your brand is about low prices (such as Wal-Mart®: Save Money. Live Better.), then it is your brand's job to find ways to continue to be congruent and consistent with that promise.

Southwest Airlines is built on the premise that it offers low fares on air travel. There is a certain expectation around the experience of the product. However, it didn't stop there; Southwest Airlines continues to be the leader in cost containment throughout the entire operation of the company; not to mention that it even dedicates a specific budget geared toward research for developing more efficient ways to fly. It developed the winglet apparatus that saves over 30 percent in fuel costs. They have come up with other efficiencies in administration, operation, training, etc. The company supplements the low-cost experience with an environment of humor that keeps its loyal customers laughing and light-hearted and ultimately creates a memorable event.

So depending on the power of your product features, differentiators, or the service experience you are promising (consistently) within your brand's DNA, then by all means, the value is there. Just like when you buy a business-class versus a first-class airline ticket, your expectations rise when you pay more for a product or service. And many people are willing to pay for an elevated level of experience.

In fact, the myth "My customers' just want the best price" is challenged by a statistic that says, "Consumers spend up to 10% more for the same product with better service" [2] .

Duane Knapp, author of *The BrandMindset*® states that "Consumers perceive that they pay in three important ways: time, money and feelings."[3] Price alone does not drive your customer's behavior but rather the consistency in how your brand delivers value.

When you think about it, how many times do you like changing vendors or brands from a product or service that you use frequently and grow to trust? A perfect example for a woman is when she finally finds a hairdresser who knows how to cut, color, perm, or style her hair just right! She wants to stick with that person as long as she can because of the consistency and the value she places on the experience. And she will pay almost anything to have that faith and trust that she will come out looking great! There's nothing worse than a bad haircut that you have to live with for four weeks! So what would happen if her stylist raised the price another $5? Think about the stress of finding a new hairdresser—one who gets her type of hair and needs—is simply not worth it. In other words, the value-added the stylist brings to her piece of mind is worth the price increase.

Look all around you. You'll see all kinds of companies who charge premium prices, and they command them, because of their strong brand experience. Take Whole Foods®, for example. They have created a revolutionary grocery shopping experience accessible to everyone in the communities they serve. Their site (www.Wholefoods.com/values) openly and proudly displays the following core values:

- Selling the highest-quality natural and organic products available.
- Satisfying and delighting our customers.
- Supporting team member excellence and happiness.
- Creating wealth through profits and growth.
- Caring about our communities and our environment.
- Creating ongoing win-win partnerships with our suppliers.
- Promoting the health of our stakeholders through healthy eating education.

The discussion of core values in chapter 1 is critical to tie in the development of the brand experience for the customer. These core values for Whole Foods set the stage for ensuring the powerful differentiators of their shopping experience versus their competition. For example, from selling the highest-quality foods to satisfying and delighting their customers at every touch point to committing to their communities and surrounding environments; it is all manifested from these values. You can see now how all the preliminary work we've done with Meg ties into everything she is doing to continue the building of her brand and its customer experience.

Whole Foods is distinguishable, notable, and growing fast with this set of core values and most importantly is living those values on a moment-by-moment basis. It has been listed in Fortune Magazine's *100 Best Companies to Work For.*

## Your Customers Seek Products/Services

So the question is: "What do you promise to your customer that is relevant in their experience and to your value?" How can Starbucks command sometimes more than $4 for a cup of coffee that you can purchase at a convenience store for one-quarter the price? What is the difference between shopping at Nordstrom versus Macy's department stores, flying Southwest Airlines vs. United, or Google vs. Yahoo!? What is the *experiential difference,* and do you promise that difference consistently?

More and more studies show that the perception of value (or lack of it) comes from the behaviors or service promise a company offers. "Value" ultimately stems from a collection of perceptions throughout the pre-, during, and post-transactional experiences. As consumers and business owners, we value relationships, fairness, trust, integrity, follow-up, and honest communication. We also seek excitement, humor, thrills, wows, and warm fuzzies! How can these elements be incorporated into what you and your employees create for your customers—both B2B (business to business) and B2C (business to consumer)?

Here are some examples from companies who have figured it out:

> —**Macaroni Grill**® (www.macaronigrill.com) servers introduce themselves and write their names upside down in crayon on the table "cloth" so you can read and remember it! (relationship)
>
> —**Ritz-Carlton**® (www.ritzcarlton.com) pleasantly surprises you by anticipating your needs and desires (and delivering on them), through constant, careful observation and documentation during your hotel stay. (wows and trust)
>
> —**Blockbuster**® (www.blockbuster.com) employees greet and acknowledge you verbally as you walk in the door and salute/thank you as you exit. (relationship and warm fuzzies)

By and large, customers interpret your employees' behaviors as your company's behaviors. Remember, we experience through our senses. There is no other way human beings can take in information, categorize, and make decisions, other than through our eyes, nose, touch, ears, mouth, and that sixth sense, intuition. So how do you take your brand and assimilate it in a relevant, consistent, and distinctive way through each of the senses? Have you ever thought about how you, as a brand, smell? How does your brand make others feel? How do you taste? These are truly serious questions you should be asking yourself. How does your brand's promise show up through the senses? Are you consistent? Are you living your values and style through the senses?

## Building Relationships with Your Customers Is More Powerful Than Price

This is where we first advised Meg to carefully craft and compose a Magic Story for Ecologé (see exercise in part II). The brand's Magic Story outlines the creation (how the company came to be), its purpose (why it is in business), and its vision (what it aspires to become) in a colorful, descriptive story that speaks to human emotion.

This will do several things for Meg and the Ecologé brand:

1. Realign her thoughts with her Brand DNA development. You can never revisit your DNA enough! Getting the DNA engrained in your mind and your employees' minds is the quickest way to begin seeing impactful results in the way your brand thinks, acts, behaves, serves, and attracts customers!

2. Articulate in story form all the amazing details of the evolution of the brand, its rooted passion, and the benefits to the customers. This is where major "ahas" happen! The detail within the story reaffirms the passion and reengages the employee culture. It creates a more three-dimensional history, roots, and a powerful way your employees get to know the brand at a deeper level. It provides them with a sort of memory of where the brand came from, how it evolved, and how they can be a part of its continued legacy.

3. Provide a powerful, emotional method for Ecologé to connect with and educate its customers—creating ROL (return on loyalty)!

4. Allow for the story to continue to evolve as Meg's company evolves, adding turning points, activities, awards, etc., for the lifetime of the company.

The second piece of advice we provided to Meg was to conduct a *touch-point audit*. This audit will help her identify all the different ways she and her customers connect (the phone, e-mail, Web site, invoicing, in person, etc.). Then we will once again refer back to the initial work she did on the creation of the Ecologé DNA. Her DNA will guide us in developing the most powerfully distinctive yet congruent behaviors and enhancements she and her team can add to her customer touch-point delivery protocol.

"Brand messaging has to be more than "market-speak," it has to be a mantra, the cornerstone of a strategy that is communicated to every member of the company repeatedly, clearly and fervently. It has to be a concept so crystal clear, so absolutely unambiguous, that there can be no questioning what it means. Every single member of the company has to have it on the tip of their tongue—and, infinitely more important, embedded deep within their beliefs. That's the only way it can be consistently spread through the thousands and millions of interactions and conversations that make up the new brand mosaic."

—Gord Hotchkiss,
President of Enquiro,
a search engine marketing firm,
January, 2007

The Brand Ascension Group also advised Meg to compose a brief yet hard-hitting customer feedback survey on Ecologé's service experience and administer it (via a third party) to her top fifteen customers. This will help her uncover some of the service-experience gaps and reveal the true perceptions (good and not so good). She can also test the Ecologé brand promise statement and other components of the entire Brand DNA (style, values, standards, and differentiators) and get valuable feedback as to whether the Ecologé brand is truly living up to its promise to her external market.

The survey initiative is another important customer touch point that needs to be thought through and carefully orchestrated.

Here's an approach to consider using an independent third party, an approach we perform for many of our clients.

- We help the client select those key customers who represent small, medium, and large purchases and those who have been long-term, medium-term, and new clients.
- We help choose a small yet thoughtful gift to provide as a heartfelt thank you for their time in responding to the survey. We recommend that the gift be delivered prior to the actual transaction of the survey. Another option is to enter the respondent's name into a drawing for a $100 gift certificate.
- We develop an appropriate number of specific, succinct, and compelling questions. We keep it as brief as possible (fifteen to

twenty-five items that may include both multiple-choice/closed-ended and open-ended questions and that takes ten minutes or less to complete) to assess how well the client is performing relative to its defined Brand DNA and product and service quality and to uncover opportunities for improvement.

- We invite the customers (via e-mail, phone, or mailed letter) to participate in the feedback process, stressing the purpose and importance of the survey, the confidentiality of their specific responses, and the gift offer.
- We conduct the survey through one or more means—electronic collection through a reliable source (e.g., Survey Monkey™, Zoomerang®), personal interviews, or some combination. We highly recommend that a third party facilitate the survey as the client will feel more comfortable and generally be more candid with an objective party.
- We compile and analyze the data, providing both quantitative and qualitative summaries.
- We create action steps resulting from the data, which fulfill the exposed gaps and work on continuously enhancing and leveraging the areas that are positive.

We believe that, for business owners, knowledge is only power when it is applied. By capturing valuable feedback from your customers, you can invent distinctive behaviors that fill in the perceived gaps in service quality and how well you are performing relative to your Brand DNA. If done well, this can only enhance positive perceptions in the minds of your customers.

We have experienced enormous "ahas" from clients who have incorporated this type of Brand Diagnostic™. You know the saying "We don't know what we don't know." The resulting data is extremely revealing and is a powerful tool to identify highly targeted actions (as it is based off of solid evidence) rather than relying on guess work as to what you think you need to be doing. The data exposes areas of opportunity and the low-hanging fruit that can drive profits. It is a focus tool to keep the company on track and constantly in tune with customers' perceptions and how well you are living your unique Brand DNA, Platform, and Promise.

# CHAPTER 6

## Myth: Branding is only Essential for Big Business

*Greatness, it turns out, is largely a*
*matter of conscious choice.*

*—Jim Collins,*
*Good to Great,*
*HarperCollins Publishers, 2001*

## THE CHALLENGE

"Hi Suzanne. Glad I was able to catch you," Meg said into her cell phone while she walked to her car.

"Yes, Meg, what can I help you with? It sounds like you're on the road. I'm going to put you on speaker phone," I said as I clicked "send" on a completed e-mail reply and reached for a notepad and pen.

"Well, I just came from my accountant's office; we're putting together a strategic plan for budgeting next year, and I presented to her my ideas on establishing a budget for our branding initiatives and then a budget for marketing," Meg said.

"My accountant asked me why I was working on branding at this stage of the business and not focusing my efforts on a simple advertising/marketing plan. She commented that branding initiatives were usually only found in the strategic plans of her larger corporate clients. And I couldn't, at least as good as you would have, give her a substantial answer to justify or at least appease her," Meg said with confusion.

"First, I want to thank you for calling!" I said as I waved Carol into my office. "And know that you are welcome to phone us anytime! Carol just came in to join us on this call," I quickly added as I pushed the speaker phone button.

"Hello Carol. Glad you are there too!" Meg said.

"Hi Meg. Thanks," Carol said as she pulled up a chair near my desk phone and seated herself.

"We love clarifying these sorts of perceptions, Meg," I continued, "because we are focused on creating a much higher consciousness of understanding the power of branding, educating our clients, and inspiring them to grow as much and as fast as they desire," I said encouragingly. "This isn't the last time you will encounter some of these types of questions from colleagues, co-workers, and vendors. There are many misconceptions of the concept of branding in the business arena. Usually it's because of the way the majority of business owners perceive the process of growth and how it is approached," I commented.

Meg agreed, "I totally get what you are saying! All this is so new to my way of thinking, and I love it. The all-too-familiar marketing push philosophy, however, has been engrained in me from my corporate position. We constantly had to have one or more advertising campaigns running in not only electronic but print media to feel like we were making the right efforts to grow our business. I don't even remember the term branding coming up! So bear with me and my ignorance!"

"You're not alone, Meg," Carol assured. "It is a process of truly understanding the power of branding—by, again, remembering the true definition of a brand: a perception that lives in the minds of your employees and customers that is based on emotion and is experienced through your products and services (including your behaviors).

"A great example of starting early with the branding 'due diligence' is when, early on, Chipotle® defined itself, its beliefs, and behaviors through an amazingly articulate manifesto. Writing this manifesto was integral to define its own brand through a story and provided a powerful road map for it to follow through the stages of growth. It solidified who it was as a company and how it would go about delivering on its product through its employees, environment, and service protocols. Then, of course, the rest is history!"

"So when you think about it," Suzanne added, "why should only larger businesses be concerned about creating a perception for their employees and customers to experience? Wouldn't all businesses, regardless of size or need, want to create a consistent perception that helps them stand out from their competition? Large, successful businesses didn't get there without fully and clearly understanding their distinct brand attributes. They understood the importance of values, of defined standards, and of understanding their brand's unique style and differentiators."

"Of course," Meg said with increasing interest. "It doesn't matter what stage my business is in. In fact, I'm thinking the sooner the better it is for any business to get a grasp on the concept of branding! I remember Carol's remark earlier when I started this journey with you on building my brand DNA. She said that I have to 'put a stake in the ground' and continue to trust the process and be as conscious about my brand as possible."

"Exactly. That's where we're coming from. Remember, your brand is your business. And the Ecologé brand's message must be crystal clear and articulated through your internal behaviors first. This strategy assures that you are prepared to deliver your products and services at a level that upholds your brand's intended perception in a consistent, distinctive, and relevant way.

"You know, another great example to use when you speak with your CPA is the successful start-up and branding of Hewlett Packard®. College pals Bill Hewlett and Dave Packard started in a one-car garage in Palo Alto sixty years ago. They had a mere $538 in start-up capital, funded from sources like Lucile Packard's secretarial position at Stanford's registration offices. They were engineers, new to building a business.

"Immediately they decided to create a corporate protocol called the 'HP Way,' consisting of cultural standards and management style attributes. Their approach was founded in respecting personal autonomy and corporate decentralization. By systematically nurturing employee satisfaction and morale, their employees led them to innovate and deliver a steady stream of leading-edge, highly profitable products. These specific behaviors, philosophies, values, products, and services kept them highly consistent and on track with creating distinction in their marketplace," I added.

Carol jumped in too. "Creating and implementing conscious brand strategies for your company takes more *time and commitment* than actual expense. And the more time and attention you focus on working ON your business rather than IN it, the quicker you will be able to secure powerful brand-relevant behaviors through your systems and processes. And this in turn will be expressed by you and your employees and experienced by your customers. These experiences will create the distinction you need for your competitive advantage."

Meg replied, "This makes so much sense. I'm trusting more and more in the process. I believe my team is ready to create those powerful behaviors. What are the steps to begin the process?"

"You've actually already started the process through the development of the Ecologé DNA," I reminded Meg. "Remember the standards you created? I specifically remember the one where you focused on making sure your employees received thorough hands-on training in the 'green' philosophies of the company and its products."

"Oh, yes, our standards of performance throughout our brand's scorecard. Let me see if I remember the areas of the scorecard: customers, processes, employees, and financial," recalled Meg.

"Exactly," I confirmed. "There was also a great standard you developed to focus on your customers; remember? It revolved around providing a 100 percent satisfaction guarantee, personalized service, and complimentary samples of differing products with every order! We will help you develop those details and flesh out your brand-congruent behaviors that will create a lot of tangible expression for your brand. I'll send you an e-mail with an exercise in it to get started!"

"Great!" Meg said. "We'll get right on it! I want to have a billion-dollar business like HP!"

"That's the spirit!" I cheered. "The fastest way to get there is to define, create, and build your brand in the early stages and let it guide you through your growth. Getting you and your team's arms around this now is critical to creating the momentum and synergy for rapid growth and implementation."

"I can envision it now!" Meg said confidently.

"Let's schedule a consulting meeting next week," said Carol, "and we'll review your homework."

**SEE PART II: READER EXERCISES, CHAPTER 6 EXERCISE, for ASSESSING AND ALIGNING YOUR BEHAVIORS TO YOUR VALUES exercise, and Ecologé's final outputs.**

## CONSULTANTS' CORNER

Many small to mid-sized companies look at strategic branding strategies as something to which only larger organizations can allocate time, money, and effort. Thus their mindset is stuck in the thought that their business-growth strategies have to revolve around their marketing budget and developing that magic campaign that works miracles and makes their businesses a million-dollar-plus revenue generator. Well, we hope that our above scenario with Meg sheds a bit of a light on that particular thought process and how that kind of strategy can put and keep you in the red now and for years to come.

What needs to be considered again and again is your overall Brand DNA. We cannot mention this enough, because your DNA is your road map to follow in every area of your business—employees, customers, processes, and financial. (See the Brand Scorecard model, Figure 6.1.) When you have completed your DNA you have all the powerful attributes right in front of you that will dictate how your company shows up in every behavior and in every area of the business, internally and externally!

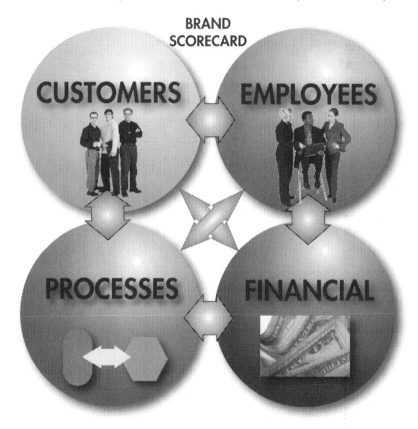

Figure 6.1

Remember that the process of branding is the defining and living of the message that in turn gets marketed to your audience. Your message is made up of brand vocabulary, brand style, brand standards, and brand values. These are your brand's specific ingredients that make it distinctive, relevant, and consistent. Since branding is all about creating perception, surely you must agree that the perceptions of small to mid-sized companies are just as important to the owners and customers as they are with larger companies. All large companies started small and then grew. Many have become who they are because of their attention to aggressively and proactively sustaining their brand (brand management).

Brands have human qualities. This is what makes the relationships work with their customers—real relationships, sprinkled with emotional decisions, history, trust, and relevancy.

Consider another once small, single-owner confectionery started by Joseph Draps. He introduced Belgium to his brand of chocolate, Godiva, in 1926 with a small retail shop on a cobblestone street in Grande Place. Draps perfected a unique formula of rich chocolate with unparalleled smoothness. With a remarkable eye for detail, he set forth the standard for Godiva's innovative selection of elegant, European, shell-molded designs and beautiful packaging. Through the years, these standards have been maintained as assiduously as Draps' recipes have been guarded.

As a result of this adherence to Draps' heritage and brand, Godiva Chocolates evoke the greatest in confectionery excellence. The same careful attention to quality is apparent in the exquisite European-style gold seals and handcrafted seasonal packaging that have earned Godiva a reputation for design excellence.

The Godiva brand was the first to create the concept of premium chocolate. Godiva did this by combining a fabulous consistent product, remarkable retail environment experiences, simplistic advertising, sophisticated, elegant packaging, and selective distribution. Godiva's standards of excellence included maintaining the product's high quality by requiring special handling during storage and display. Its growing popularity as a premium product is because of its innovative approach in careful manufacturing, elegant, brand-relevant advertising, and packaging (www.Godiva.com).

Creating specific perceptions that are congruent with your Brand DNA, Platform, and Promise can begin simply with altering internal (employee) behavior; a powerful, under-utilized strategy that is too often overlooked and under-leveraged in the small-business environment. Yes, this means training, communicating, observing, and delivering a way of being that is distinctive throughout the customer experience.

In *Branded Customer Service*, authors Janelle Barlow and Paul Stewart state "Human behavior is the primary means of brand reinforcement within the realm of customer service."[1]

How much does it cost to change a behavior? The answer is more about soft dollars in the form of time than actual hard dollars. Changing behavior is a matter of communicating the necessary, revised expectations, mapping the behaviors out, and practicing them so that the new behavior becomes second nature and conscious within the delivery of products and services to your customers. The sooner you begin this process, the faster the perceptions will build and attract your perfect customers, create loyalties, build referrals, and increase your overall bottom line!

**EXAMPLE**

One of our favorite clients runs a premier tanning salon. Through several secret shopper exercises and a variety of controlled focus group studies, we came to the conclusion that tanning is considered to be a commodity in the mindset of its customers. We helped our client create a powerful yet simple customer touch point:

*A new customer who signs a six-month contract for tanning service receives a personalized guided educational tour of the facility and equipment; a complimentary bottle of premium indoor tanning lotion of her/his choice; and a pair of required protective eyewear.*

During this process a personal relationship is built between the employee and the customer, a bond that is rarely cultivated elsewhere. This is just one of the many behaviors it invented from its DNA that guides its behavior and value positioning in the minds of its clients. So,

*EVERYTHING YOU DO IN YOUR BUSINESS
EITHER CONTRIBUTES TO OR TAKES AWAY
FROM THE PERCEPTION OTHERS HAVE OF YOUR BRAND!*

To drill down this point a bit further, let's introduce the "7-11 rule". This rule states that within the first seven seconds of contact with your brand, your customer forms eleven impressions. These impressions come from all the ways we as human beings take in or receive information. What are those ways? Through our senses: sight, sound, touch, taste, smell, and don't forget, our intuition! So when you think about these eleven impressions your customers are forming, the question is what are you doing in those first seven seconds to help control those perceived impressions? What does your Brand DNA define for your brand that you can use to shape the experience of those first seven seconds…and for every second thereafter?

In *The BrandMindset®,* Knapp says "At the end of the day, a brand is only that which is perceived in the consumer's mind, or what we denote as the mind's eye. The consumer's mind's eye is influenced by thousands of impressions daily and changes often."[2] Remember, if you don't create, build, and manage the perception of your brand, your customers will. And if they are allowed to control the perception, it will probably be tagged onto a previous or predisposed (usually negative) experience they had somewhere else, something over which you had no control.

So why not take the reins of your own brand's experience? Define and create it now so that your brand shows up in a very tangible and experiential way to your customers. You can begin to design your brand to show up consistently and relevantly. When this is done, you will begin to build a powerful history with your clients, a history that more than likely will create purchase traditions and embed a sense of ritual. Wouldn't it be the ultimate to have your customers thinking of you in terms of a firmly rooted habit in which they engage often? And with undying loyalty to your brand, your customers serve as an external extension of your internal sales force. And here's the best news … you don't have to pay them!

Now there are always those die-hard workaholics who feel that running a small business should be a struggle. If you proudly tout that:

- it should be hard,
- requires a 24/7 consumption of your time,
- includes major ups and down swings,
- involves ongoing reconnaissance and strategic planning to lure in your customers and you must reinvent yourself every six months.

Then you will continue to struggle. However, if you are determined to:

- work smarter, not harder,
- attract and retain the best employees,
- have fun in your business-building process,
- attract and keep perfect, loyal customers,
- create some amazing behavioral differentiators,
- operate more consistently,
- increase your brand value positioning,
- increase qualified referrals,

- be completely authentic in how you show up,
- decrease customer price sensitivity, and
- increase your marketing dollar's ROI,

… then keep reading and do the exercises for the key learning points in each chapter as outlined in part II to transform your brand!

# CHAPTER 7

## *Myth: My Brand Appeals to Everyone*

*When a customer asks you to lower your prices,*
*provide a service that you don't truly want to*
*provide, or does not appreciate what you have to*
*offer, remember that is not your perfect customer!*
*—Stacey Hall & Jan Brogniez,*
*2001, Attracting Perfect Customers*

## THE CHALLENGE

The elevator climbed from P2 of the parking garage to the lobby level, the doors opened, and there was Meg waiting for a lift up to the eleventh floor, which housed the Brand Ascension Group's offices. "Well, hey there! What timing. Can you grab these books for me?" I asked.

Meg's eyes were wide with curiosity as she stepped inside the elevator, the doors closed, and she replied, "Hi Carol. Absolutely," and took the three hardcover books and four magazines out of my left hand.

I still had a large tote bag on my left shoulder, a rolling computer bag in my right hand, and a purse on my right shoulder, but I heaved, "Phew! Thanks for the help! I didn't realize I had so much to bring to the office today."

"It's the least I could do. Wow, what's all this for?" Meg inquired.

"It's research for an upcoming speech I'm doing at a major trade show. I have to stay on top of my game all the time with the latest data and research available. Anyway, enough about that, are you ready for today's session?" I asked.

"Absolutely. I'm looking forward to it. You and Suzanne are always such an inspiration for me. Every time we meet I grow by leaps and bounds. By the way, I wanted to tell you how wonderful these last few weeks have been with you both taking impromptu phone calls from me at the last minute. I can't thank you enough for making yourselves available for so many issues that have come up when I needed some advice," she replied in a warm and genuine tone.

*She really is growing by leaps and bounds,* I thought. I then replied equally as warmly, "It's part of who we are and how we show up as a brand. In fact, one of the brand standards we have established for BA Group requires that we are 100 percent present and available in our delivery of on-the-spot, value-added services to our clients."

The elevator chimed and the door popped open as we reached the eleventh floor. There was Suzanne standing at the reception desk just outside our small group of executive suites. She looked our way and said, "The conference room is ours for the rest of the afternoon." She then came over to greet us, and I jokingly said, "Suzanne, we're going to have to start charging Meg extra for all her impromptu phone calls of late."

"Aahhh! Cha-ching," reinforced Suzanne with a wink to Meg. The three of us laughed as we made our way to the conference room just off the lobby reception area.

We settled in, and I pulled out three bottled waters from the small fridge in the conference room. I opened the session with, "Meg, you did a great job on this last homework assignment. What you have accomplished here will most definitely streamline our work in helping you establish more detail and rigor around the standards and the performance levels you will adhere to for your customers, employees, processes, and the financial areas of the business."

"Oh, thank you for that feedback! I was hoping I'd do well on this assignment. It's interesting—once I started working on my homework and thinking about more detailed standards and actions to support my Brand DNA, I realized that I'm in a real dilemma."

"Oh? And how so?" Suzanne replied.

"Well," Meg began with a deep sigh, "you know my overarching standard is '100 percent guaranteed satisfaction and personalized service.' I have a lot of ideas on more detailed standards and actions to support this. However, over the past two weeks I have spent at least half my time working with this one new prospect, testing my initial ideas on the standards for customers, and I just can't seem to please him. I'm desperately trying to secure a contract with this prospect."

Meg clasped her hands, stretched her arms out in front of her, and then stood up and sighed. "Besides my time, my sales rep from the West Coast has put in as much if not more time on this deal, and we can't seem to come to an agreement on anything with him. This is so huge for us in terms of the business we would generate from this account. We have struggled with trying to secure a major client in the boutique resort market ever since I started Ecologé. This could be our first big break." Meg paused a moment and then paced the floor looking a bit weary while obviously in deep thought. I could sense that she needed to vent a bit, so we gave her a bit of space.

Meg continued, "This prospect has five major resort hotels throughout the United States, one opening in Mexico this year, and another slated for Asia next year. They're the biggest prospect we've come across. We've gone back and forth with him, helping him understand what we are all about, what makes us different from every other body-care company, and trying to understand what they are looking for."

Her voice began to pick up speed and crack. "We've provided him numerous and plentiful samples of our products, conveyed to him the unique ingredients and properties of our line, and revised our quotes based on his continual requested changes, not to mention tiptoed back and forth on price so we could find the right number that's win-win. Oh, and on top of all that, this morning they hinted that they are considering a competitor of ours, but they won't tell us who. After all we been through, we're just now finding this out. We suspect the competitor is Diva Skin Care, which is a lot bigger company. We're small fry in comparison, and they have a totally different philosophy than ours. And they're not green at all."

"So what does that tell you?" Suzanne asked.

"That this prospect is beating us down at every opportunity, and I'm not sure he truly appreciates the 'green' philosophy upon which our products and brand were founded. But we need this account; we need this account!" recounted Meg. She collapsed back into the seat of her chair with a hand on each side of her face and braced her head with her elbows on the conference room table. She looked at Suzanne and then to me. "What do I do?" she pleaded.

"Hmm," I said. "In our last session and in your homework you have come up with some great ideas built around your standards in which you mentioned testing the waters with this prospect."

"And as you can see, we have clearly bent over backward trying to impress upon this one prospect what we are all about. What do we do when they don't share the same philosophy or appreciate our standard of excellence, which is the bedrock of how we deliver in a simple, pure, elegant, and personable way?" replied an exasperated Meg.

Suzanne stood up and walked over to the window. In a reassuring tone, she turned to Meg and asked a very pointed question in her typical, direct style that compels our clients to dig deeper to find the answers within. "Meg, what's most important to you in determining if a customer is a good fit for the Ecologé brand?"

Meg thought for a moment and then replied, "Finding the customer who appreciates what we offer and how we offer it and who truly values what we are all about. We pride ourselves in our commitment to the type of ingredients that our products reflect: natural and organic, pure and simple, being in harmony with nature rather than abusing it. We allow the creation of personal experiences that restore and balance the mind, body, and spirit."

Suzanne drilled deeper. "Have you defined your ideal customer? Do you know an ideal customer when you see one?"

"Well … not in definitive terms, but since you asked, I would say that our ideal customer is one who values all that we're about and wants to pass this on to others. They appreciate what we stand for, our style and values, our standards of excellence, pure and natural ingredients. They appreciate the type of products we offer because we care about the positive effect they have on our customers."

"Does this prospect, however important they may appear to be in growing your revenue base substantially, reflect anything of what you have just articulated?" I interjected in an inquisitive yet matter-of-fact tone.

Meg sat erect in her chair as she squeezed both hands into fists with a grimace on her face and in a squeaky, almost whining tone said, "Oh, you both are doing it again; helping me to see the obvious that I haven't wanted to face. I'm more concerned with trying to win this prospect over than ensuring they are a good fit for what my brand is all about. I want to have a big break into the resort market, but I know deep down that this is not the ideal customer. I guess it is not that much of a dilemma after all! Why can't he appreciate what the Ecologé brand is all about? I've spent so much time spinning my wheels. And how do I attract the right customers to my brand? How do I find them?"

"Build it and they will come!" Suzanne and I blurted out in perfect unison.

Meg relaxed her body as she eased back in her chair, closed her eyes, and smiled. In an almost self-reprimand she said, "Yes, I remember. We've discussed that in a previous session. Ugh, what have I *not* been thinking and doing?"

"Now take a few deep breaths," I said. "You've got to be crystal clear on who your ideal customer is. Once you are clear, it will be much easier for you to qualify and attract the right customers into your 'brand's space.'"

Suzanne interjected, "Think about the time and energy you and your sales rep have spent the last two weeks on this one prospect that doesn't fit your brand when you could have spent time 1) nurturing your 'A' customers, 2) asking for their referrals, and 3) following up with other prospects in the pipeline that better fit your brand."

"You've obviously got a lot on your mind, and we've got a lot of work to do this afternoon, Meg," I said as I opened my portfolio and pulled out my papers. "How about we focus on one step at a time and first get to work reviewing your last homework assignment. Then we'll discuss a process for you to use in defining your ideal customer. This will include developing a strategy to begin qualifying and attracting those customers that fit your definition—build it and they will come!"

"Sounds good to me," she said in a relieved tone.

**SEE PART III: READER EXERCISES, CHAPTER 7 EXERCISE, for your DEFINE YOUR IDEAL CUSTOMER exercise and ECOLOGE's final outputs.**

# CONSULTANTS' CORNER

So many businesses try to make their brand appeal to everyone who knocks on their door. If a brand appealed to everyone we would have neither contrast nor competitors in our market. The reality is that brands are more appealing when they are highly focused and deliver exceptionally well to a specific market and clientele.

### Target Market

Consider these brands and their target markets:

- ESPN® focuses on the sports-minded enthusiast versus the non-sports-minded couch potato.
- Whole Foods® wants consumers who eat a naturally healthy diet of the highest quality and who care about taste and nutritious foods in their purest form versus those who indulge in foods high in fat, cholesterol-laden with partially hydrogenated oils and other highly processed ingredients.

- Nutrisystems® has carved out a niche menu that appeals to men and is differentiating itself from WeightWatchers® and Jenny Craig®.
- Apple® appeals to those who appreciate the sense of design, creativity, and innovation in the look and feel of its products.

Not everyone who drives a truck prefers a Chevy. Some prefer a truck made by Ford, Toyota, or another brand for that matter. Harley-Davidson has a strong cult-like following of Harley diehards, yet there are people who much prefer the ride of a BMW bike. Consider the major car manufacturers. Until recently, General Motors had numerous brands and models to choose from all targeting a variety of different consumer needs and desires. Think about the differences in the target markets between a Chevrolet and a Cadillac and the choice of various models within each of those brands and how each appeals to the different needs and lifestyles of consumers.

## Brand Focus

Think about your unique brand and what you are all about. According to Brad VanAuken, author of *Brand Aid*, the true power of a brand lies in its focus.[1] At the Brand Ascension Group we couldn't concur more about the power and importance of focus. By focusing on who you are and appealing to your specific target customer or market segment, you can generate much better leverage to distinguish yourself. You can specifically target a customer group that matches your brand's values and messages and reflects the essence of what your brand stands for.

We also believe that it is important to stay true to the essence of your brand to attract customers into your brand's space. Don't try to be something you are not. Most businesses are started because there is some passion behind the founder in what they are doing and what they envision. This can be a service or product that fills a need or gap or improves one's way of life. Over time, so many businesses lose sight of that passion or why they are in business. Many entrepreneurs get caught in the trap of trying to grab every customer they can so they can make as much money as they can in the shortest time possible. In the process they spin their wheels and waste a lot of energy, time, and money trying to appeal to everyone in the market.

Consider the following experience scenario:

Chapter 7

You join a friend for dinner and drinks at a local martini bar and restaurant. You find that it is themed and decorated nicely (a Frank Sinatra "Rat Pack" style club environment), but when you sit down at the table and review the menu you find a variety of items that don't connect to the theme.

You order a chicken Caesar salad and find mandarin oranges in it, not to mention that the romaine lettuce is somewhat wilted and the Caesar dressing tastes pretty bland, nothing like a true Caesar, more like a generic brand from the local grocery store. The martini you ordered, however, is pretty good. Then you realize, halfway through the course of your dining experience, that the genre of the music has changed several times from country to pop to light rock with no connection to the theme of the club. You see a poster on the wall advertising Karaoke on Thursday nights. The incongruence becomes more magnified. You notice that the servers are dressed in jeans and either tank tops or T-shirts. Even worse, their behaviors exhibit none of the refined, suave qualities you might expect to reflect the theme and style of the establishment—again a real disconnect. You say to yourself, *what is happening here? Do these people even know who they are?*

You converse a bit more with your friend and are then approached by the owner, asking if you would like dessert, to which you reply, "No thank you." He seems like a well-intentioned businessman. You then ask him why the music keeps changing. He says he is trying to accommodate the varying requests of his customers. You think to yourself, *what's really happening is that he is trying to appeal to everyone.* With these actions, the experience in his establishment is a mish-mash. He is only diluting the value of the brand experience by not committing in total to the authenticity of the theme. During your brief conversation with him, he admits that he has a variety of customers who are not regulars and that he'd like to build a solid customer base. Hmmm … you know he churns them left and right. The club leaves no distinction in your mind, you wonder why he is still in business, and you vow never to venture back in again!

## No Brand Is Universal

Need I say more? No brand is universal! It is a nice thought, but not every brand appeals to everyone. Furthermore, why would you want your brand to appeal to everyone? Can you imagine how difficult it is to satisfy everyone? You can't! When you try to be all things to all people, you spend a lot of time spinning your wheels, and the result is a dilution of rather than an increase in the value of your brand.

Not even powerful brands like Harley-Davidson, Nordstrom, Coca Cola, Pepsi, Ford, Chevrolet, Starbucks, Apple, or GM try to appeal to everyone. The learning point is that there has to be a difference between your brand and your competitors' brand that provides a positive contrast. The positive contrast gives you a huge opportunity to create distinction in the mind of your market.

We conducted a brainstorming session with Meg to help her clearly define her target market based on her Brand DNA, the distinctive attributes of the Ecologé brand essence and messages—all as a reflection of the market she wants to serve.

Be consistent, relevant, and distinctive according to what your brand stands for and leverage these characteristics to appeal to your target market.

## CHAPTER 8

## *Myth: The Size of My Marketing Budget Determines My Brand's Success*

*Advertising budgets will continue to be slashed because credibility and trust are not built with advertising like they were in the past. Today's customers, investors, and other key audiences are more skeptical than ever before.*
—*Mike Paul, President and Senior Counselor, MGP & Associates PRAs, quoted in brandchannel.com, "A Branding New Year. Several branding experts share their predictions for 2007," February 12, 2007, by Alycia de Mesa*

## THE CHALLENGE

It was 9:37 AM when the light flashed on the telephone console, indicating that an incoming call was about to come through. I picked up the phone and answered, "Good morning, the Brand Ascension Group. Carol speaking."

"Hi Carol," said Meg on the other line. "Hope I have caught you at a good time."

"Yes you have. By the way, can you still make our appointment this afternoon?" I inquired.

"Oh, yes," she replied in a bit of a frenzied tone as I picked up some background noise through the phone. It sounded like Meg was talking to someone else as I overheard her say, *"Please let her know I'll phone her back as soon as I finish this call."*

"What's the matter, Meg? I sense of bit of agitation in your voice."

"Well, you know me oh too well now, don't you? Since you asked, I'm feeling a bit stressed at the moment. I need to work on my budget and business plan for next year. In fact, that was my accountant calling. I'm getting pressure to give her a first pass at a budget by tomorrow. We had a long discussion about the marketing section of the overall budget yesterday. She's insisting that I allocate 10–12 percent for marketing expenditures next year; quite a bit more than last year. She keeps saying that I must have a bigger budget for marketing or I won't realize my growth goals. I'm not sure what to do. I don't really have enough information to confirm or refute what she is saying other than I know instinctively that I need to have some sort of marketing budget!"

*Oh, here we go again,* I thought to myself. *It is one thing for a marketing person to feel so strongly about the marketing budget, but it's very interesting hearing it said by an accountant.*

"And I sense that the discussion with your accountant on her recommendations makes you a bit uneasy and you are trying to reconcile in your mind whether you need to justify that level of expense?" I asked.

"You got it!" she retorted.

"Meg, can you delay your accountant another week so we have some time to discuss this? We can include it in our agenda for this afternoon's session with Suzanne," I replied with enough insistence to convey the importance of my request.

"Yes, I think I can delay her, even though she's putting the pressure on. I'll tell her that I need more time. She'll understand if I say I'm trying to get my arms around what expenditures I'll need and that I don't want to be premature in my projections without thinking them through," she said.

"Great. See you in a few hours."


It was 1:30 pm when I greeted Meg in the reception lobby. "Hello there! Meg, you are right on time as usual! We'll be meeting in the conference room. Suzanne is preparing some water and an assortment of teas and other beverages for you."

"Oh, I'd love some of that exotic apricot tea you all have. It's so fragrant," she said. "It's just the remedy to relax from a hectic morning."

"Absolutely. We still have a bit of it left in our stash! We want you calm, clear of mind, and relaxed for our session!" I replied with a smile as we entered the conference room.

"Hi Meg," said Suzanne. "Looking forward to our session?"

Meg replied, "Definitely!"

I then lifted the small jar of "Stress Less" Inhalation Beads off the table and passed it to Meg. "Here, take in some of your own remedy to relieve some of that stress while I get your tea brewing."

"Thanks Carol." Meg opened the sample jar she had left a few weeks ago in an earlier session, took a whiff, and sank into one our cushiony chairs at the conference table. Looking at the package, she said, "This stuff is great!" She read the information on the label out loud:

> *Take the vapors in:*
> *Active essential oils of Lavender,*
> *Chamomile, and Sage extract work naturally to reduce the*
> *daily stress and tension of life. Breathe it all in, letting your*
> *senses inhale nature's own remedies. Benefits the mind, body,*
> *and spirit!*

"That's exactly what I need!" she said. We finally settled in with a cup of tea and got down to business.

"By the way," Suzanne said, "congratulations on firing that prospect we talked about in our last session and finding a great new customer that fits the bill. Carol and I always have a sense of resolve and commitment to our brand when we say no to someone who doesn't fit our client profile!

Meg laughed. "Oh, I feel so silly now. I fretted for weeks trying to please them. I just let 'em go, and the next day I got a call from this company called Lotus Spa Resorts insisting that they meet with us. They weren't even on our radar screen. They had received a referral from not just one but two of our existing customers who raved about our unique products and personalized service. It was so reaffirming. We've been trying hard to put in place some key processes that enable us to be more of who we already are as a result of going through the Brand DNA. It's taken some work, but we're getting there!"

Suzanne interjected, "Doesn't it feel good to put your time, money, and effort into building the infrastructure that supports and drives your business, nurturing your existing customers rather than spending huge amounts of marketing and advertising dollars without ever really knowing your return on investment?"

"Absolutely!" Meg said. "I have to trust in the process that if we serve our existing retail customers well, the payoff will be huge. It will mean more business from them as they continue to grow and from their referrals of us to others. They are truly a source of inspiration for us when they become our raving fans! Wouldn't it be great not to have to worry about marketing to new customers and just let our existing customers bring the referrals to us?"

"So how does it feel when you speak to a referred contact versus a cold call?" I said.

Meg paused and then chuckled as if remembering a situation in her mind and responded, "The whole tone of conversation with a referred client versus one we are pursuing is so different and such a pleasure! The referred client has a preconceived thought about who we are, and it is very positive. With a cold-call prospect, it feels like you have to constantly prove yourself and sell them on your unique differences."

"Right on! And that brings us to the priority area of discussion, your marketing budget!" claimed Suzanne.

"Yes, we need to discuss it pronto!" insisted Meg. "Sonja, my accountant, means well. She has been a good partner for me. Not to mention that she's been looking after my financials since I started Ecologé and helped me through some difficult times. I don't know what I would have done without her."

"We have no doubt that she means well. Each advisor to you plays a key role in your business based on their expertise," replied Suzanne.

I stood up from my chair and walked over to the white board, picking up a dry erase marker, and said, "The question you need to ask yourself, Meg, is not how much you should allocate to marketing. Rather, the question is what areas of branding and marketing efforts will be required to create the internal infrastructure and then the appropriate, congruent messaging for your brand awareness. This will better support your revenue goals so you can create a sustainable growing business. We're not suggesting that you have to choose one over the other, as there is a place for both marketing and branding in your budget. What we want you to think about is this:

> *Marketing* comes from a *"state of lack,"* whereas
> *Branding* comes from a *"state of being and knowing."*

I emphasized key words attached to "state." "It is a difference in mindset. What I mean is that with a marketing mindset one is predisposed to feeling that they are lacking in something, whereas a branding mindset promotes a state of confidence in knowing you are doing the right things by focusing and building the brand with a holistic and balanced perspective. Which mindset do you prefer?"

"Well, certainly, the obvious mindset for me after all I have learned from the two of you is that of branding, but does that mean that I shouldn't think about marketing? I have to have some budget for marketing."

"Absolutely. We would never ask you to eliminate the marketing budget. There is a need for certain well-planned marketing activities; for example, a press release creates good exposure but costs very little. As you've already learned from us, it is not the size of your marketing budget that determines the success of your business but rather the investment in your internal branding efforts that create consistent, relevant, and distinctive brand experiences. Remember the three most powerful attributes of highly successful brands?"

"Umm ... ahh, they're on the tip of my tongue," Meg said, struggling to remember. "Oh, yes, I remember that consistency and distinctiveness were two of the three."

"Here's a hint to the third," said Suzanne. "It starts with 'R'!"

To which Meg replied, "Ahh, yes, relevance."

Suzanne reminded Meg of the definitions:

- **Consistent:** Showing up the same way every time. Walking the talk and being true to your Brand Platform and Promise.
- **Relevant:** Matching/satisfying internal and external messages and values and ensuring congruence with your Brand Platform and Promise.
- **Distinctive:** Standing out uniquely and decidedly different from your competition in every way and congruent with your Brand Platform and Promise.

She explained again, "You want to invest in creating consistent, relevant, and distinctive multisensory experiences. Remember the research we covered in the Brand DNA session from the author of *Brand Sense*, Martin Lindstrom?"

"Oh, yes," Meg answered. "In particular I remember how you said Singapore Air leverages its Asian heritage. Its flight attendants reflect the exotic and beautiful native women as an extension of its brand. It leverages Asian style music in commercials, its Sing-Air airport lounges, and in the airplane cabins before takeoff."

"Exactly, and it has developed and patented a distinctive floral scent that the flight attendants wear and that is also infused in the cloth towels each passenger receives as they enter the cabin before takeoff. It leverages the senses down to the minute details. I experienced the sensory elements of the brand consistently when I lived and worked in Asia," I said.

"Singapore Air is creating powerful sensory experiences that are congruent with the core values of its brand and the overall essence of what it stands for," added Suzanne. "This in turn cultivates the emotional bond its customers have with its brand."

"Now back to the issue at hand. Again, I repeat, it's not the size of your marketing budget that counts, but the investment in the brand infrastructure that determines your success. We suggest that you consider what is known; in other words what marketing activities will be needed, such as collateral replacement, business cards, your newsletter, public relations, sample products for trade shows, gifts to potential prospects you identify or who express interest to you in your products and services, and perhaps advertisements you may want to place in some trade magazines, podcasts, e-mail notices, etc. You also know that your Web site and other e-mail marketing activities will require some funding to better leverage your presence in the market based on our initial assessment. Also, let's not forget about leveraging virtual technology! We'll put you in touch you with the guru of virtual meetings."

Suzanne explained, "Very importantly, you will need to consider expenses required to build the internal infrastructure, such as the new point-of-sale software program for when you set up your first retail location next year. Don't forget the personalized service training that will be required when you hire new employees so they are oriented to the Ecologé way of being and doing business. What systems and processes will be required of you and your team to enable you to deliver on your standards of performance?"

I added, "We'll need to consider the investments you'll need to make to ensure that you hire the right people when you open your new retail outlet. That's a huge step, moving into bricks and mortar for the retail piece of your business. What type of pay and benefit programs will you need for these employees? What sensory experiences will you create to capitalize on the unique qualities of your brand and create an emotional bond with your employees and customers? Think about all the touch points and the opportunities to leave a lasting and memorable impression—how will you close any gaps between perception and reality? Remember what we said in the Brand DNA session? Being conscious about your brand is the key to managing it. Always put yourself in your customers' shoes and experience your business through their eyes, ears, nose, hands, etc."

"So there will be costs involved," said Meg. "And this is all a part of the internal branding piece that is so vital to the success of my business. Wow, this is a lot to consider."

"That's right!" reaffirmed Suzanne. "There will be both hard- and soft-dollar costs. Most important, it is about being conscious of every detail in managing and delivering the Ecologé brand experience. If your way of being is not consistent, relevant, and distinctive with your marketing message, your customers will not bond with you and your brand. In fact, if you are not consistent, you will only erode confidence in your brand. All the money you put into your message will be wasted if it is not backed up by the customer's experience with your brand."

I added, "Our advice is to keep your marketing message and efforts simple and true to what you are as a brand and begin building the internal pieces to ensure that truth and consistency. You have to start somewhere. We suggest at this point we do two things. First, list out your must-haves and your wish list based on what we know today, estimate some ballpark costs, and then prioritize based on cost and potential impact—the biggest bang for your effort! You can then work all of it into a consolidated budget for branding that includes your marketing expenditures as a subset. As more information becomes available, you will delve more deeply into your priorities and what the business needs. You can then reallocate dollars accordingly within that overall budget as you progress forward. Make sense?"

"Phew ... that's a lot to think about!" she said. "I know that I need to build the internal infrastructure to support my marketing message down the road and need to lay it all out. I'm so glad I have you all to help me think through this."

"Second," said Suzanne pushing forward, "we strongly encourage you to begin leveraging the senses to build and affirm the perception of and create congruent experiences with your brand. Because of the nature of your brand, you have so many opportunities to leverage sight, sound, taste, touch, smell, and intuition. You are all about mind, body, and spirit. We'll want you to take the initial work you and your team brainstormed in the Brand DNA session and then begin to develop ideas to more fully leverage the senses. That will be your homework assignment, to go back and brainstorm with your team following today's session."

"Right!" I said and moved toward the flip chart. "We have our work cut out for us today." I tore several sheets from the flip chart and taped them to the walls. "We need to list everything out on paper so we can see it and prioritize."

**SEE PART II: READER EXERCISES, CHAPTER 8 EXERCISE, for your LEVERAGING THE POWER OF THE SENSES TO BUILD YOUR BRAND EXPERIENCE exercise and ECOLOGE's final outputs.**

# CONSULTANTS' CORNER

Well, there you go! Again, we know that marketing has an important role in building some businesses!

Our experience shows that it is not what you spend in marketing that keeps customers coming back but rather the sensory experience they have when buying your products and services.

### What Is the ROI on Your Marketing Investment?

Here's a good example. Think about the much acclaimed Super Bowl ads. Companies spend millions of dollars on these ads for a thirty-second commercial spot. It is like it is a competition as to who can come up with the most funny, provocative, or catchy ad. Yet, for many of them, you can't even remember what the product is.

Marc Gobé, author of *Emotional Branding,* wrote in a *Business Week* article:[1]

> It seems that the more emotionally disconnected brands are from their consumers, the more they feel they need to spend on advertising ... when the commercial becomes more popular than the product, you really have a problem—not least that it doesn't serve your brand long-term.

So what is the learning point here? The learning point is you have to question the ROI (return on investment) if the consumer can't remember the brand or be compelled to take action. So be smart about investment of your marketing dollars!

Do you ever see advertisements for Starbucks? Rarely. You might see an occasional billboard when it is test marketing or introducing a new product, or perhaps an occasional advertisement from time to time. Instead, Starbucks invests in its infrastructure and the creation of multisensory, tantalizing experiences that keep its customers coming back for more. Not just capitalizing on smell and taste, but touch, sight, and sound as well—through the look and feel of the interior of its stores. Most people feel good when they leave a Starbucks—that's capitalizing on the intuition sense! It invests significantly in its employees as well. The company took two very bold and unheard-of actions during a time when corporations were going through significant shifts to deliver greater returns to shareholders—it offered part-time employees a generous benefits package and introduced the first-ever stock option program, called "Bean Stock," to all employees, making them partners. We all know how successful Starbucks is. It is a multibillion dollar company not to mention the perfect example of a brand that has built its success from the inside out!

Another of our clients spent quite a lot of money on a promotional campaign that met with disaster. The misfire? It did not effectively communicate or train its employees relative to offerings in this campaign. Guess what happened? The promotion caused a lot of confusion with customers. The promotion negatively impacted customer confidence in it, eroded trust, and negated the goals of the entire campaign.

## Commit to What You Promise

The attraction of consumers to a brand is much more than a marketing exercise. Companies often allocate huge amounts of funds for the marketing budget touting the value proposition to their market. They often do a good job of attracting new customers only to find that they are spinning their wheels because their customers are exiting as fast as they come in, sometimes faster! Customers find themselves disappointed when the brand doesn't live up to the expectations created in those marketing messages. Consider commodity industries like the airlines and banking. They peddle marketing messages that are supposed to differentiate themselves from competitors only for the consumers to be totally disappointed. For customers and employees, after all those promises, there is little change in the service levels or distinctive sensory experiences.

Companies spend numerous dollars on their marketing messages only to set themselves up for failure because they haven't created a solid internal infrastructure to deliver on those messages. They realize that they are not living up to those expectations, and in fact it creates indifference in the customers' minds as to whether to do business with them, and yet they continue to bandage the issue with more marketing messages. What they should be doing is investing the time and money in the internal workings of their leadership, culture, systems, and processes and creating powerful sensory experiences—the drivers of creating solid relationships with customers. And by the way, if you are in a commodity market, you have a huge opportunity to differentiate your brand in the way your people deliver on the brand.

The Gallup organization conducted a poll of six thousand consumers between November 1999 and January 2000. They found that the people (employees) in an organization were by far the most important driver of brand loyalty. They reported that in the airline and banking industries the influence of people was a significant driver of brand loyalty. Customers were ten to twenty times more likely to repurchase from those organizations with outstanding employees.

## Internal Branding Experiences

Authors B. Joseph Pine II and James H. Gilmore note in *The Experience Economy* (1999) that brand experiences are events that engage individuals in an inherently personal way and they actually occur on an emotional, physical, intellectual, and even a visceral level.[2]

So if you remember one thing, it should be that the size of your marketing budget doesn't determine your brand's success. Your business is a stage, and you must design memorable sensory events for your customers. To do this, you must have the internal infrastructure in place. In order to inspire your customers, keep them coming back for more and generate more business through their referrals, you must first inspire your employees by creating memorable sensory events for them so they better understand and believe in your brand, your products, and your services and how they can better represent and be true brand advocates.

According to a study conducted by Jack Morton Worldwide, employees want live experiences—preferring meetings and events second only to contact with an immediate manager. 86 percent agreed that live experiences are more engaging than other forms of communication. Live experiences lead to action, with 84 percent believing that they are more likely to influence behavior/performance. 86 percent agreed that live experiences will make them more likely to talk positively about the company they work for with others. So start with the internal—your employees—and build your brand from the inside out!

> Think about this ... what is your brand's leave-behind or legacy?
>
> People will forget what you said,
> They will forget what you did,

But they will never, never forget how you made them FEEL!

—*Maya Angelou*

Think about the leave-behind or legacy at every touch point and how you show up in a sensory way of expressing your brand that is consistent, relevant, and distinctive.

# PART II
# READER EXERCISES

# CHAPTER 1 EXERCISE

## *Identify and Define Your Core Values and Style Attributes*

There are three parts to this exercise. Part A includes the identification of your core values. Part B includes the identification of your brand's style attributes. Part C consists of developing a brief definition for each of your values and style attributes. You will find Ecologé team's outputs within each part.

**TIME TO ALLOT:**
*Allow 30–45 minutes for part A; 30–45 minutes for part B; 45–60 minutes for part C. This is well worth the invested time. (Schedule an official appointment in your calendar with your team, and get commitments to attend the meeting.)*
**PROPS:**
*Flip chart, markers*
**WHO TO INCLUDE:**
*A team of three to seven is preferred, from different areas of the business (e.g., customer service, administration, sales, etc.). If you are a start-up business or you have no employees, rally your trusted advisors, colleagues, business associates, friends, and family to assist you in generating ideas for this exercise.*

## INSTRUCTIONS

### Part A: Identify Your Brand's Core Values

When a business is in alignment with what it stands for, it shows up more authentic and consistent. When we live by our values, we reinforce what our brand stands for to our employees, our customers, and the communities/markets we serve. When we don't live by our values, we lose good will and erode relationships with others as we don't show up authentic to what we say we are. As mentioned in Chapter 8, values are not behaviors in and of them but rather are a reflection of something we say we are and what has true meaning for us. Alignment to what your brand stands for occurs when your values match your behaviors. We call this "Cognitive Resonance." If companies espouse certain values but the behaviors don't match, there is misalignment in the minds of your customers. We call this "Cognitive Dissonance." The actions create the potential for mistrust.

The following is an exercise adapted from Tony Schwartz, author of *The Power of Full Engagement.* Let's start with those guiding principles that must be essential to everything you do to begin to uncover your *brand's true values*. First answer the following three questions:

1.  List three or more qualities you can't stand when you see them or experience them in other businesses.

    _____    _____    _____

    _____    _____    _____

### *Ecologé Example:*

> *Non-"green" Practices Wastefulness*
> *Arrogance    Inefficiency    Lavish*

2.  List three or more qualities you are embarrassed about when they surface or occur within your business.

    _____    _____    _____

    _____    _____    _____

### *Ecologé Example:*

> *Bickering    Over-complication    Lack of attention to detail*

3.  List three or more qualities that your business emulates when you are performing at your very best.

    _____    _____    _____

### *Ecologé Example:*

> *Eco-Awareness  Simplicity  Moderation  All Natural*

4.  Using the answers to questions 1 and 2 previously, list the positive of the words you identified in the space below. Your new list will be contrary to what you wrote and represent what you truly stand for.
    List positive words for those in questions 1 and 2 here:

    1.  _____    _____    _____

    2.  _____    _____    _____

**Ecologé Example:**

| | |
|---|---|
| **Green practices** | **Sparing** |
| **Humility** | **Efficient** |
| **Simple** | **Pure** |
| **Harmony** | **Detailed** |

Now do the following:

- Consolidate any of the above "opposite" words that are similar to each other. For example, if you chose honesty and integrity, they are close in meaning. Decide which of the two is more accurate to what your brand values. List the resulting set of remaining "value" words in the first column below.

- In the second column, identify their level of importance on a scale of 1–7, with 1=Lowest and 7=Highest. Then circle only the top three and no more than four based on their level of importance. Rating the level of importance is a "sanity check" to ensure if it will hold up to the test of what your brand stands for. Remember that your value words should be written in a tense that can be placed in the statement: "We value _____."

**List Value Word**

**Rate Importance of Value**
**1= Lowest**
**7= Highest**

1. _____     _____

2. _____     _____

3. _____     _____

4. _____     _____

5. _____     _____

6. _____     _____

Select the top four of the highest-rated values and record them in your Brand DNA template.

***Ecologé Example:***

| List Value Word | Rate Importance of Value<br>1= Lowest<br>7= Highest |
|---|---|
| 1. **Green Practices/Environmentally conscious** | 7 |
| 2. Efficient | 6 |
| 3. Humility | 5 |
| 4. **Purity/All Natural** | 7 |
| 5. **Simplicity** | 7 |
| 6. Moderation/Sparing | 5 |
| 7. Detailed | 6 |
| 8. **Harmony** | 7 |

Based on the ratings above here are Ecologé's final chosen brand value attributes:

- Environmentally conscious
- Purity
- Simplicity
- Harmony

Set the above aside for a moment.

## Part B: Identify Your Brand's Style Attributes

Now do the same for your style attributes. To begin to uncover your brand's style attributes think about the manner in which you want to present yourself to others; in other words, your distinctive brand personality. Answer the following two questions using adjectives as a descriptor. (Example: warm, engaging, bold, vivacious, exuberant, determined, diligent, and adaptable are adjectives. Notice how they outline personality traits.)

1.  What specific style attributes show up in your "attitude" as a brand, your quirks and/or the manner in which you present yourself, your products, and/or your services? List the terms (using adjectives—i.e., words that describe or qualify nouns or pronouns, as these evoke emotion) you believe describe your style, but be honest. Don't list something you are not.

    _____  _____  _____

    _____  _____  _____

*Ecologé Example:*

| | | |
|---|---|---|
| *Elegance* | *Progressive* | *Personable* |
| *Friendly* | *Confident* | *Savvy* |

2.  What would others who know your brand—customers, employees, suppliers, community, etc.—say about you when describing your "unique way" or "manner of being?" Ask three to five of these key observers for their input and list them below and compare them to your list in question 1. (Note: Be sure to ask them to describe you in the form of adjectives—words that qualify or describe a noun or pronoun and that evoke emotion.)

_____   _____   _____

_____   _____   _____

### *Ecologé Example:*

**Chic**          **Avant-garde**          **Approachable**
**Persistent**    **Well-informed**

Consolidate any words that overlap or are similar (decide on one or the other word) under questions 1 and 2 above and list in the table below as follows:

- In the first column, list all remaining words.
- In the second column, rank how often they show up within your business as your unique style on a scale of 1–7 with 1=Least Often and 7=Most Often.
- Then circle the top three or four highest ranked words. In the case of a tie, you must break the tie. Any more than four will only dilute your ability to leverage your most distinctive style attributes.

| Style Attributes (adjective form) | Rate How Often the Style Attribute Shows Up: 1=Least Often, 7=Most Often |
|---|---|
| 1. _____ | _____ |
| 2. _____ | _____ |
| 3. _____ | _____ |
| 4. _____ | _____ |
| 5. _____ | _____ |
| 6. _____ | _____ |

This is the first step to create alignment and gain the trust needed for your customers to be loyal to your brand!

Select the top four of the highest-rated style attributes and record them in your Brand DNA template.

*Ecologé Example:*

| Style Attributes (adjective form) | Rate How Often the Style Attribute Shows Up: 1= Least Often; 7= Most Often |
|---|---|
| CHIC/ELEGANT | 7 |
| AVANT-GARDE | 6 |
| PERSONABLE/FRIENDLY | 7 |
| APPROACHABLE | 5 |
| SAVVY/CONFIDENT | 7 |
| WELL-INFORMED | 5 |
| PERSISTENT | 5 |

**Based on the ratings above here are Ecologé's final chosen brand style attributes:**

- Chic
- Avant-garde
- Personable
- Savvy

## Part C: Define Your Brand's Value and Style Attributes

Every word in our language has a connotative and a denotative meaning. That is why it is important to specify your brand's meaning of these attributes so that every stakeholder involved in the brand comprehends its intention through the definition. Now begin to think of the characteristics that reflect the descriptive qualities of your style, values, and Brand Platform. List each of your previously identified core values and style attributes and define their meaning. Describe the meaning using crisp and succinct statements.

When composing your definition for each attribute, we recommend that you stay away from the "Webster" definition but rather think about how your brand perceives each term and how you live (or want to live) the attribute within your specific environment.

### *Ecologé Example:*

**Values Definitions**

- **Environmentally conscious:** *Conduct business with a "green" philosophy by educating ourselves and our customers on the importance of using only biodegradable products (ingredients and packaging).*

- **Purity:** *Offer only certified organic and natural products of the highest-quality elements of nature: herbs and flower essences, essential oils, natural sea salts, etc.*

- **Simplicity:** *Minimalist packaging and containers to preserve the delicate balance of all ingredients and serve as a natural expression of their essence.*

- **Harmony:** *Act in concert with nature by preserving the natural balance of mind, body, and spirit.*

**Style Attribute Definitions**

- **Chic:** *Simple elegance to reflect a refined and stylish yet minimalist look and feel to how we visually show up in our packaging, on our Web site, in our marketing collateral, and in personal dress in representing the brand.*

- **Avant-garde:** *In pursuit of distinguishing characteristics that reflect unconventional and progressive attitudes: we intend to "push the envelope" in thought, form, and substance.*

- **Personable:** *Warm and engaging behaviors that reflect the friendly and approachable nature of all our associates in our interactions with one another, our customers, and the communities we serve.*

- **Savvy:** *Confident, well-informed, and knowledgeable; our products and research will ensure that customers receive the finest botanicals and elements of nature.*

Now use the space below to define each of your core values and style attributes.

**Definitions:**

## VALUE DEFINITIONS

1. _____:

_____

_____

_____

_____

_____

2. _____:

_____

_____

_____

_____

_____

3. _____:

_____

_____

_____

_____

_____

4. _____:

_____

_____

_____

_____

_____

## STYLE DEFINITIONS

1.  _____:

    _____

    _____

    _____

    _____

    _____

2.  _____:

    _____

    _____

    _____

    _____

    _____

3.  _____:

    _____

    _____

    _____

    _____

    _____

4. _____:

    _____

    _____

    _____

    _____

    _____

5. _____:

    _____

    _____

    _____

    _____

    _____

Congratulations! You're on a roll now. Don't stop—building your brand is right around the corner! Exhibit 1 on page 151 is a template for documenting your Brand DNA. Use this template to write in your differentiators and standards in the sections provided and that you identified in the exercises for chapter 2.

## MEG'S BREAKTHROUGH

After a break during the Brand DNA session Meg passed the following handwritten note.

*Dear S & C:*

*Wow! I can't get over how powerful and insightful this exercise on values and style has been. Talk about a whole different approach to identifying and understanding what means most to us as a brand! Obviously, the disparities we uncovered reveal a lot. For instance, I got to thinking about our value of environmentally conscious and realized of course that to be true to this we must only use environmentally friendly recycled and natural products for the ingredients and packaging. We have to be 100 percent authentic.*

*I can't wait to get back to the office to implement the first set of changes that will fuel the right behaviors and set our brand afire! I'm chomping at the bit for the rest of this session!!*

*M* ☺

# CHAPTER 2 EXERCISE

## *Define Your Differentiators and Establish Standards for Your Brand*

There are two parts to this exercise. Part A is the identification of your differentiators; part B identifies your standards. You will find the Ecologé team's outputs within each part.

### TIME TO ALLOT:
*Allow 30–45 minutes for part A and 90 minutes for part B. This is well worth the invested time. (Schedule an official appointment in your calendar with your team, and get commitments to attend the meeting.)*

### PROPS:
*Flip chart, markers*

### WHO TO INCLUDE:
*Team of three to seven are preferred; from different areas of the business (e.g., customer service, administration, sales, etc.). If you are a start-up business or you have no employees, rally your trusted advisors, colleagues, business associates, friends, and family to assist you in generating ideas for this exercise.*

## INSTRUCTIONS
### Part A: Define Your Differentiators
*Discover Your Brand Differentiators to Enhance Your Competitive Advantage.*

In this next exercise, you and your team will have the opportunity to dig deep into your business and discover what truly authenticates your brand. These details will allow you to clearly articulate the distinction between your brand and your competition. Your *differentiators* are skill sets and quality attributes that distinguish you from all others in your industry category.

Your differentiators can include your unique approach to servicing your clients (e.g., holistic, balanced, synergistic, highly customized, careful assessment, planning, and follow through). They could include your unique mix/blend of talent, such as your degrees, certifications, years of experience, vastness of experience, awards, etc. Think of all the core assets your people have to bring to the "credential" table and to exemplify/demonstrate your brand. Then hone in on those differentiators that truly set you apart from others in your industry category/market space.

## IDENTIFYING YOUR UNIQUE BRAND DIFFERENTIATORS

1.  Make a copy of the list of differentiating considerations outlined below for each team member.
2.  Give your teammates several minutes to review the list above and make notes.
3.  Begin the brainstorming by asking for ideas of your true differentiators based on the areas listed.
4.  Write down the ideas from the group on a flip chart for the next fifteen minutes. Keep asking for more. Ask them to clarify further what they mean by their statement to give the rest of the group more to work from. When you have discovered at least five powerful and true differentiators, continue to provide as much detail as you can pertaining to each, with numbers, statistics, and other specifics that support the differentiator statement. Note: The categories below are designed to help you think through and identify true differentiators for your brand. It is not expected that you will have a differentiator under each category. If you cannot quantify a differentiator, then move on to the next category (e.g., 6 exclusive and premium wines from the Coonawarra region of South Australia; 95% of materials used in our packaging are recyclable.)
5.  When you have agreed to the final drafted differentiators, write them in the space allotted.

**Make a copy of this list for your team.** Answer the following targeted "distinction" questions to help identify your unique brand differentiators:

**Let's start with your brand differentiators.** These are the specific skill sets and attributes that *enhance* what you bring to the business and *distinguish* you from your competitors. Consider the following categories of questions and identify as many differentiators as you can think of:

1. **MARKET SOLUTIONS (points of difference):** What "pain" points (i.e., problems) are you solving for your market, and what is unique about the way you do it?

2. **COMPETITIVE SPACE:** What are your strengths and weaknesses compared to your closest competitors? Can you make those strengths more apparent? Think about what differences in perception we might have between these brands occupying the same fast-food industry: Wendy's vs. McDonald's vs. Burger King vs. Sonic vs. Carl's Jr.

3. **SOCIAL and WORLD CONDITIONS:** How is your brand responding or not responding to these conditions? How can you leverage a particular current condition, perception, or event with how your brand responds or solves issues?

4. **DUPLICATION DEFENSE:** Can someone easily recreate, imitate, or copy your point of difference? Even though having your competition replicate you is the best form of flattery in some ways, be conscious of these areas of differentiation and constantly enhance them.

5. **SUSTAINABILITY:** Do you have unique points of difference that have been sustained long-term, get more valuable with time, or become outdated quickly from style trends, innovation, technology, or nuances in cultures?

6. **DISTINCTIVE OR ONE-OF-A-KIND SKILL SETS:** Think about identifying the unique quality attributes of your services or products, your environment, delivery, credentials, awards, etc., that distinguishes you from all others in your industry category (i.e., no one else can lay claim to how you do it!).

7. **PROPRIETARY/INTELLECTUAL CAPITAL:** What has your brand solely developed or even enhanced and currently leverages? Consider technology, trade secrets/patents, processes, systems, software, words, phrases, methods, products, and people.

8. **UNIQUE BEHAVIORAL ACTIONS**: What behaviors do you possess and demonstrate that are uncommon in the industry and set you apart from your competition?

9. **ABUNDANCE/LACK of SOMETHING:** Do you have the widest or largest varieties of a certain product? Are you fulfilling an industry gap with select or hard-to-find products? Do you fulfill a unique service gap? Find ways to capitalize on these differentiators.

10. **UNIQUE HERITAGE/HISTORY:** Your business was founded on a certain heritage or "way of being" (Native Indians, Amish, etc.) or your business was founded at the beginning of a new era, etc.

11. **REACH or EXCLUSIVITY:** Do you have a unique breadth of clientele? Or are you highly exclusive in your clientele?

12. **AWARDS:** What awards has your business won that makes you stand out?

13. **EMPLOYEE CULTURE:** What distinguishes your brand internally? Do you have a unique employee culture, award structure, benefit structure, rituals, behavioral differences from your competitors, etc?

14. **ASSOCIATION:** Is your brand associated with any organization outside your industry that creates a sense of greater belonging (e.g., American Heart Association, Breast Cancer, St. Jude's, Environmental Causes, Wildlife Conservation, etc.)? How are you leveraging that association and involving your employees and customer/clients?

## *Ecologé Example:*

1. **MARKET SOLUTIONS (points of difference):** Seven exclusive R&D partnerships. These partnerships have won the most awards in their field of expertise. Our use of rare, organic rain forest botanicals is a point of difference.

2. **COMPETITIVE SPACE:** We are the number-one leader in breadth of expertise credentials.

3. **SOCIAL and WORLD CONDITIONS:** We contribute 3.5 percent of our profits to the Botanical Environmental Coalition.

4. **DUPLICATION DEFENSE:** We have two unique extracting processes to patent through our partners who produce for us.

Developed unique customer-service processes that ensure long-term relationship nurturing through streamlined database technology and frequent personal connection.

5. **SUSTAINABILITY:** Hopefully, our processes will enable sustainability and point of difference, but more and more companies are entering the market; few do it like us. Use 100% recycled packaging for products.

6. **DISTINCTIVE OR ONE-OF-A-KIND SKILL SETS:** 93 percent of product line is organic; striving for 100 percent. Our exclusive partnerships provide us access to the best and brightest minds (award-winning certified herbal specialists, botanists, etc.).

7. **PROPRIETARY/INTELLECTUAL CAPITAL:** Two unique production processes. These are proprietary for us and under contractual NDA.

8. **UNIQUE BEHAVIORAL ACTIONS**: We guarantee our products 110 percent. That means if our clients are not satisfied, they can return our product for 110 percent of their money back or get the same amount in credit toward other Ecologé products.

9. **ABUNDANCE/LACK of SOMETHING:** Lack: we have 0 percent synthetic or chemical ingredients in our products.

10. **UNIQUE HERITAGE/HISTORY:** Still a young company; however, we will always have an organic product line and will leverage that over time.

11. **REACH or EXCLUSIVITY:** Published in 13 magazines. We currently sell to over thirty-seven hotels/resorts/spas and our products are sold in twenty-three retail outlets.

12. **AWARDS:** Working on submission to industry competitions, local BBB customer service excellence, and Fortune Small Business Best 50 of the Year.

13. **EMPLOYEE CULTURE:** Every employee contributes .5 percent of their salary (not mandatory, but encouraged) toward an environmentally focused not-for-profit organization of their choice and is encouraged to spend one paid day per quarter volunteering for their selected not-for-profit organization.

14. **ASSOCIATION:** Same as employee culture response.

## ECOLOGE'S FINAL LIST OF DIFFERENTIATORS

- Exclusive partnerships with highly reputable and award-winning certified herb specialists, botanists, biologists, ecologists
- Contribute/donate to Botanical Environmental Coalition
- Importers of rare, organic-certified rainforest botanicals
- 93 percent of product line is all organic
- Two proprietary production processes
- 0 percent synthetic or chemical ingredients
- Four eco-educators in our field of expertise
- Two patented extracting processes
- Employees contribute .5 percent of salary toward "enviro" causes
- Published in thirteen magazines
- Use 100 percent recycled packaging for products

As you can see from the above, Ecologé has dug deep to determine their unique, authentic differentiators. They took the time to dissect each differentiator topic and listed potential unique qualities and then worked on applying numbers, statistics, and or metrics to whatever they claimed that was factual and fleshed out their true competitive advantage for this snapshot in time.

They have committed to reviewing their differentiators at least every twelve months. Differentiators, along with standards, are part of the innovative and dynamic side of your core Brand DNA, which means that these are the areas that change and evolve based on how the brand is evolving within its own industry. Make sure you commit to reviewing your Brand DNA differentiators on an annual or semi-annual basis so that you can take full advantage and leverage what makes you different and creates your ongoing competitive advantage.

**Your Turn**

Now take some time to think about your brand and the unique and distinctive capabilities that enhance what you bring to the business you are in. If you have employees, schedule at least one hour with three to five of them to help brainstorm where your brand can capitalize and leverage the differentiator categories listed above. If you do not have employees, bring together some trusted advisors or business associates to help you brainstorm.

Use a flip chart to brainstorm on the differentiation categories listed on page 124 and 125. Remember to focus on where you can attach numbers, statistics, or metrics to your differentiators. Your brand may not have a unique differentiator in each of the listed areas. Choose the areas you have a definite competitive advantage and focus on getting highly detailed in those areas. Then list your completed unique brand differentiators below.

1. _____

_____

_____

_____

2. _____

_____

_____

_____

3. _____

   _____

   _____

   _____

4. _____

   _____

   _____

   _____

5. _____

   _____

   _____

   _____

6. _____

   _____

   _____

   _____

# PART B: ESTABLISH YOUR BRAND STANDARDS

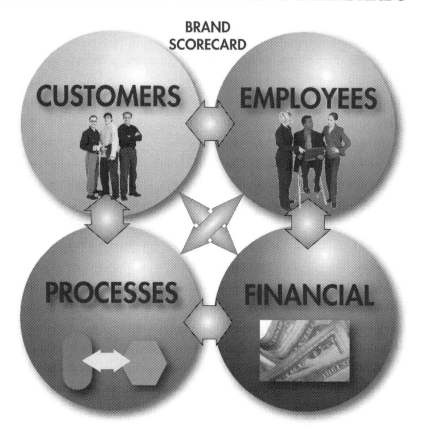

Take a look at these four quadrants of your Brand Scorecard: employees, customers, financial, processes. Your task is to review your core values and develop an overarching standard for each area of the Brand Scorecard. Consider all your values when composing your overarching standard. Then detail out how each overarching standard will be exemplified through a series of supportive actions. What specific actionable behaviors must be in place to live up to and sustain your overarching standard in each area of the business and assure they are congruent with your brand values and style?

> *During this exercise, remember to tap into your core values to assist you and your team in forming the overarching standard for each area of the business along with their supportive*

actions. *Everything you come up with should be linked in some way to your Brand DNA values.*

## Instructions for Completing Your Brand Scorecard Standards

1. Brainstorm with your team the overarching standard for each area of the business (Brand Scorecard: customers, employees, processes, and financial). Remember that your overarching standard should exemplify a "normal and customary level of performance excellence that is reflected in your company's operational practices" (e.g., customer-relationship-management philosophy—always deliver on time; always within budget, always respond to customer requests and issues within three hours).

2. Fill in the final overarching standard in the first column in the table below relative to the area of the Brand Scorecard.

3. Review your overarching standard statement and circle the key action words or phrases to isolate the areas that will be focused on when developing your supportive actions.

4. Then in the second column to the right on the table below, identify and list at least four or more supportive actions that define what needs to be done to achieve and sustain the relevant overarching standard (e.g., What do we need to do in order to attract and develop employees?)

5. Then in the third column, identify which of your Brand DNA values relate/connect to each of these supportive actions (this helps you focus your actions on behaviors that are specific to exemplifying your values/style).

Use the following as a general guideline when considering and developing an overarching standard for each of the areas of the Brand Scorecard.

## EMPLOYEES

What overarching standard of **EMPLOYEE PERFORMANCE EXCELLENCE** will you establish and deliver consistently? The standard should:

- Be reflective of your brand values and style in action.
- Include detailed areas of consideration like hiring and training, employee feedback, empowerment, rewards, performance, and communication.

## CUSTOMERS

What overarching standard of **CUSTOMER SERVICE EXCELLENCE** will you establish and deliver consistently? The standard should:

- Be reflective of your brand values and style in action.
- Consider areas like customer feedback, service delivery/response time, communication, problem escalation/resolution, etc.

## PROCESSES

What overarching standard of **PROCESS PEFORMANCE EXCELLENCE** will you establish and deliver consistently? The standard should:

- Be reflective of your brand values and style action.
- Consider areas like product specifications, continuous process improvement, quality processes, and employee and customer satisfaction metrics and systems and should have an INTERNAL and an EXTERNAL focus.

## FINANCIAL

What overarching standard of **FINANCIAL PERFORMANCE EXCELLENCE** will you establish and deliver consistently? The standard should:

- Be reflective of your brand values and style in action.
- Consider areas like returns or rewards to employees, costs of performance (G&A), and returns to shareholders and customers.

**Ecologé Example:**
Now complete your brand standards for each area of your Brand Scorecard.

# CUSTOMERS:

## YOUR OVERARCHING STANDARD _____

_____

_____

_____

## SUPPORTIVE ACTIONS and Relevant DNA Value/Style

1. _____

   _____

2. _____

   _____

3. _____

   _____

4. _____

   _____

5. _____

   _____

6. _____

   _____

# ECOLOGE EXAMPLE:

# CUSTOMERS—BRAND SCORECARD

**OVERARCHING STANDARD**—100 percent satisfaction, "Wow" personalized service, guarantee and Ecologé percent contribution on behalf of the customer to not-for-profit partner.

**SUPPORTIVE ACTIONS and Relevant DNA Value/Style**

1. Develop and agree on specific verbiage for the 100% satisfaction guarantee (i.e., what guarantee includes); where to display on packaging, website, collateral. (SAVVY)
2. Define what personalized service is for Ecologé. (PERSONABLE)
3. Ensure documented procedures for information on up-to-date eco-friendly, green products to convey to customers. (ENVIRO-CONSCIOUS)
4. Create percent plan of Ecologé donation (for each customer purchase) to not-for-profit and follow-up plan with customer. (PERSONABLE)
5. Establish what every order is accompanied with to surprise and delight customer. For example: sample product). (AVANT-GARDE)
6. Determine what size and type of samples, how many per order per dollar value of purchase. (CHIC, SAVVY)
7. Determine continued promotion (e.g., 10-percent-off coupon on next order and pamphlet on the latest research in eco-friendly processes, botanical blends, and/or technology used). (HARMONY)
8. Create customer feedback form and process to gather info regularly with targeted improvements identified. (PERSONABLE)

## EMPLOYEES:

### YOUR OVERARCHING STANDARD _____

_____

_____

_____

### SUPPORTIVE ACTIONS and Relevant DNA Value/Style

1. _____

_____

2. _____

_____

3. _____

_____

4. _____

_____

5. _____

_____

6. _____

_____

# ECOLOGE EXAMPLE:

# EMPLOYEES—BRAND SCORECARD

**OVERARCHING STANDARD:** Hands-on learning program to understand benefits of products and the green philosophy; personal contribution, collaboration, and sharing.

**SUPPORTIVE ACTIONS and Relevant DNA Value/Style**

1. Well-documented procedural, and educational manual on all products, ingredients, benefits, and how used. (ENVIROMENTALLY-CONSCIOUS)
2. Create a training program on key elements of our "green" practices and processes to ensure that employees are well-versed on products and uses. (PURITY)
3. Establish timeline on training initiatives and updating of employee knowledge as new processes and procedures developed. (CHIC)
4. Employees receive complimentary products for self and family—encouraged to use and test. (PERSONABLE)

# PROCESSES:

## YOUR OVERARCHING STANDARD _____

_____

_____

_____

**SUPPORTIVE ACTIONS and Relevant DNA Value/Style**

1. _____

_____

2. _____

_____

3. _____

_____

4. _____

_____

5. _____

6. _____

# ECOLOGE EXAMPLE:

# PROCESSES—BRAND SCORECARD

**OVERARCHING STANDARD:** We are dedicated to creating simple, streamlined operating processes that are as environmentally friendly as possible.

### SUPPORTIVE ACTIONS and Relevant DNA Value/Style

1. Create a list of all current processes to audit. (SAVVY)
2. Review and identify processes to streamline, automate, and integrate as much as possible to create great efficiencies. (SIMPLICITY)
3. Establish a "simplicity process" protocol. (SIMPLICITY)
4. Reinvent current and new processes that affirm and enhance our value of simplicity and harmony. (HARMONY)
5. Identify and implement continuous process improvement assessment/review schedule. (SIMPLICITY)
6. Implement software program for appropriate customer-order management. (SAVVY)

### YOUR OVERARCHING STANDARD _____

_____

### SUPPORTIVE ACTIONS and Relevant DNA Value/Style

1. _____

2. _____

_____

3. _____

_____

4. _____

_____

5. _____

_____

6. _____

_____

# ECOLOGE EXAMPLE:

# FINANCIAL—BRAND SCORECARD

**OVERARCHING STANDARD:** We establish creative and progressive employee and customer incentive programs (loyalty rewards, profit pools) while dedicating a portion of our revenues to select environmental causes.

### SUPPORTIVE ACTIONS and Relevant DNA Value/Style

1. Benchmark best practices in other industries on employee and customer incentives. (PERSONABLE)
2. Identify key elements of employee and customer incentive programs. Define and document program details. Review/update contribution and incentive plans annually. (SAVVY)
3. Identify appropriate forums/partners (not-for-profits) to assign contribution plan. (ENVIRONMENTALLY-CONSCIOUS)
4. Establish criteria for contribution plan.
5. Create timeline and communication plan for rollout of both programs. (HARMONY)

6.  Create and implement metrics and process to measure bottom-line performance and internal/external brand perception. (SAVVY)

# CONGRATULATIONS!

Celebrate with your team time well spent in building your Brand DNA!

Once your overarching standard has been established for each of these key business areas, they will drive the thought process around more detailed standards that support how you deliver on your brand. Map out the supportive actions, prioritize and implement in bite-size pieces. Do a few things well before tackling more.

It is also important to affirm and reaffirm the behaviors of your staff that support the standards. Your standards need to be lived daily by your employees, and metrics should be established that reflect the standards for each area of the scorecard. You can also reinforce these standards through simple reward-and-recognition programs, which are a great way to generate collective support from staff.

In summary, remember this: once articulated and embedded, your brand differentiators and standards will provide you tremendous leverage in what you are good at and how you deliver. Again, your brand standards are a part of the "innovative" area of the Brand DNA model and require that you review and update as the brand continues to evolve into its market space. It is up to you to consciously set the bar for managing your brand!

**ECOLOGE'S FINAL BRAND STANDARDS**

**Standards**

*Employees:*

- Hands-on learning program, "green" philosophy; personal contribution, collaboration, sharing

*Customers:*

- 100 percent satisfaction, "Wow" personalized service with each order guarantee and Ecologé percent contribution on behalf of the customer to not-for-profit partner.

*Processes:*

- Simple, streamlined, automated, and integrated

*Financial:*

- Creative and progressive employee/customer incentive programs (loyalty rewards, profit pools)

## MEG'S BREAKTHROUGH

During our afternoon break after the sections on differentiators and standards, Meg pulled Suzanne and me aside for a quick check-in.

For a few moments she looked back and forth at the two of us. I couldn't quite read what was on her mind. Then she began with …

> *I can't tell you how this has totally helped me to understand more about our session at Starbucks this morning. This process is one of the best investments that could have made for my business. I am even more convinced that we need to build off of our Brand DNA.*
>
> *I can see the light bulbs going off in my team throughout this day's session, and we still have more to do. I have to admit that I wasn't sure how they would react, but now that we have gotten this far, I can see how we need to leverage our unique capabilities and develop rigorous standards in how we deliver in each of the areas of the Brand Scorecard. It seems so obvious now.*
>
> *After a brief discussion with Stefan during the last break, I've decided that one of the first areas we need to focus on is our standards for delivering to our customers. This includes establishing a way to qualify all the vendors we use to enable us to better deliver on our commitments to our customers.*

Suzanne and I smiled and nodded as we rejoined the rest of the group.

Exhibit 1 on page 151 is a template for documenting your Brand DNA. Use this template to write in your values, style, differentiators, and standards in the sections provided and that you identified in the exercises of chapters 1 and 2.

# CHAPTER 3 EXERCISE

## Discover Your Brand Platform
## and Declare Your Brand Promise

There are two parts to this exercise. Part A is the discovery of your Brand Platform; part B is the declaration of your unique brand promise. You will find the Ecologé team's outputs within each part.

**TIME TO ALLOT:**
*Allow 30–45 minutes for part A and 30*
*–45 minutes for part B. (Schedule an official*
*appointment in your calendar with your team,*
*and get commitments to attend the meeting.)*

**PROPS:**
*Flip chart, markers*

**WHO TO INCLUDE:**
*Team of three to seven are preferred; from different areas of*
*the business (e.g., customer service, administration, sales, etc.).*
*If you are a start-up business or you have no employees, rally*
*your trusted advisors, colleagues, business associates, friends, and*
*family to assist you in generating ideas for this exercise.*

## INSTRUCTIONS
### Part A: Discover Your Brand Platform

If you had three to four words to describe the overall *essence* of your brand, what would they be? According to Brad VanAuken, author of *Brand Aid*, "Brand essence is the timeless quality that the brand possesses. It is a brand's heart and soul."[1] The words you choose to reflect your Brand Platform should be crisp, constant, and enduring in your selection. Remove one word and the platform loses its meaning.

Your Brand Platform crosses boundaries and cultures. It exemplifies the most dominant characteristics of your brand. It is not a product or industry description, it is the *one constant* that permeates every aspect of your business. It has meaning that elicits positive, heartfelt emotion in your employees, and its essence is grasped quickly and easily.

Your Brand Platform is:

- Your brand "mantra"
- Your brand's fundamental *essence* and "way of being"
- A way to transcend your products and services
- Succinct and inspirational
- Derived from the most distinctive attributes of your DNA, usually three to four highly descriptive words (it is not a tagline!)

Brand Platform Samples:
- **Fed Ex:** *The World, On Time*
- **Nike:** *Authentic Athletic Performance*
- **Hallmark:** *Caring Shared*
- **Disney:** *Fun, Magical Family Entertainment*
- **The Nature Conservancy:** *Saving Great Places*

Brand Platform Examples of Brand Ascension Group Clients:
- **Engineering Firm:** *Respectful, Collaborative, Equity-Driven Visionaries*
- **Tanning Salon:** *Excellence, Simply Mind-Blowing Experience*
- **Media Advertising Company:** *Entertain, Engage, Excel! (E³)*

## INSTRUCTIONS

1. Gather your team and review your Brand DNA.
2. List your most dominant or top key attributes (usually from values and style attributes) from your Brand DNA:

_____ _____ _____

_____ _____ _____

*Ecologé Example: (most-dominant attributes)*
*Simplicity      Environmentally conscious      Pure*
*Harmony      Avant-garde    Chic*

3. Rearrange the attributes, create synonyms, and explore different combinations of the words to hone in on the terms that reflect the timeless, constant, and enduring nature of your brand's essence. Remember that every word has meaning and elicits emotion. If you were to lose a word, you would lose the total meaning.

   ***Ecologé Example: (word combinations)***

   ***Combination #1: Simple ~ Pure ~ Eco-Friendly***
   ***Combination #2: Harmonious ~ Chic ~ Avant-garde***
   ***Combination #3: Simple ~ Harmonious ~Evolving***
   ***(SHE)***

Insert your Brand Platform Draft notes below:

*FINAL BRAND PLATFORM:*

_____

*Transfer your final platform to Brand DNA template on page 151.*

## CONGRATULATIONS!
Celebrate with your team on time well spent building your Brand DNA!

### Part B: Declare Your Brand's Promise

We recommend that you take the Brand Platform exercise to your team and flip chart the values and descriptions together; then collectively use those descriptions to compose your unique brand promise. Record final notes on this sheet and then transfer them to your digital Brand DNA template.

Your brand's promise articulates your brand's *value proposition*[2] and engages everyone in the company to consciously deliver the benefits your customers and employees can expect and will experience at every touch point in doing business with you. It is a unique and specific internal "promise" written as a statement and used to adhere to as a "way of being" throughout every aspect of your business … setting the rules for doing business. The promise …

- Exemplifies how your brand pays off for someone else; how you will make a difference in the lives of your customers.
- Should reflect in more detail how your Brand Platform provides value for someone else.

The brand's promise is a concise statement or description of the core benefits your company offers consistently to current and potential customers (external) as well as describing the overall "way of being" within your employee culture (internal). The fundamentals of creating the promise statement include answering the following questions. Read through these questions and how Ecologé responded to them.

1. What business is your brand in? Think about appealing to the functional and broader emotional elements of what you provide, rather than your industry classifications.

_____

_____

_____

_____

_____

*Ecologé Example:*
- *Ecologé—in the MIND, BODY, SPIRIT business (not the consumer products/body-care business)*

*Other Examples:*
- *Southwest Airlines—in the SERVICE business (not the airline business)*
- *Starbucks—in the PEOPLE business (not the coffee business)*

2. What makes your products and services unique among your competition?

_____

_____

_____

_____

*Ecologé Example:*
- *Ingredients and processes used to manufacture*

3. How do you offer unique value to your customers? Consider the entire experience the customer receives.

_____

_____

_____

_____

*Ecologé Example:*
- *Personalized nature of our service provided at each touch point*
- *Customer education on the benefits of using eco-friendly, organic products for our planet and the wonderful effects for uplifting one's mind, body, and spirit*

4. How are your core values exemplified in your promise?

*Ecologé Example:*
- *We must deliver on our values by creating an authentic emotional experience of simplicity and harmony along with environmentally conscious practices to enhance mind, body, and spirit.*

_____

_____

_____

_____

**Your Brand Promise Composition:**

*Ecologé Example:*

> *Ecologé commits to enhancing personal harmony through simple environmentally conscious sensory activation of the mind, body, and spirit to perpetuate evolution.*

Now list your values:

**Brand values:**          **What behaviors in the business justify or support these values?**

———————————   ——————————————————————————

———————————   ——————————————————————————

———————————   ——————————————————————————

———————————   ——————————————————————————

———————————   ——————————————————————————

*Brand promise composition: (Read aloud to your team.)*

Use the values and descriptions above and the answers to the previous four questions to compose your unique brand promise. Create a clear, articulate sentence that embodies your brand's DNA and commits your brand to a way of being. Remember that your brand's promise is a declaration that articulates your company's value proposition and exemplifies the behavioral experience you commit to deliver in every interaction, business decision, and customer touch point. This promise engages everyone, both internally and externally, and sets the rules for doing business.

**Compose your unique brand promise below:** (This is the commitment to declare representing both the internal, employees, and the external, customer, levels of your business.):

———————————————————————————————————————

———————————————————————————————————————

———————————————————————————————————————

_____

_____

_____

_____

_____

Transfer your final brand promise composition to the digital Brand DNA template on page 151.

Exhibit 2 at the end of this exercise illustrates the unique Brand DNA, Platform, and Promise developed by Meg and her team at Ecologé.

**IMPORTANT:** There is one last task to complete before moving on to the next chapter exercise. Share your Brand DNA with all your employees. Make copies and post it in your office. Brainstorm ways with your team to begin embracing and emulating the Brand DNA so that you can truly begin to show up in a distinctive way.

## MEG'S BREAKTHROUGH
During our second day, Meg slipped a hand-written note to Suzanne and me.

> *What a powerful exercise! This was tough in that our team was so determined and committed to making sure we were highly conscious in the development of our Platform and Promise. We are so excited with what we came up with and feel it truly represents who we are. We are clearer than ever on what "stake in the ground" our brand is committed to! Our Platform and Promise will be a part of our lives every day here at Ecologé—in our conversations, our processes, and our culture.*
>
> *The one thing, among many, that feels so great is that I am not the only one with this passion anymore; my entire team is living and breathing this brand and has taken it on as their own. It is such a feeling of relief and support to know that my team "gets it," and I am comfortable with any one*

*of them representing who we are. This collective energy we've created is moving us toward our growth goals faster than we thought possible!*

*Once again, kudos to you both and to your amazing Brand DNA methodology!*

*Yours in full gratitude,*
*The Ecologé Team!*

## Exhibit 2

[COMPANY NAME] _____

**BRAND DNA
DIMENSIONAL NUCLEIC ASSETS®**

**DIFFERENTIATORS**

_____
_____
_____
_____
_____
_____
_____

**STANDARDS** (Overarching Statement)
EMPLOYEES

........................................
........................................
........................................
........................................

CUSTOMERS

........................................
........................................
........................................

PROCESSES

........................................
........................................
........................................

**STYLE**

........................................
........................................
........................................

**VALUES**

........................................
........................................
........................................

FINANCIAL

........................................
........................................
........................................
........................................

**Our Brand Platform/Mantra**: *your brand's fundamental essence, consistent across product categories and services, Derived from the most distinctive attributes of your DNA – usually 3 – 4 highly descriptive words. (Insert below)*

**Our Brand Promise:** *a statement that articulates your company's value proposition and exemplifies the behavioral experience you commit to deliver in every interaction, business decision, and customer touch point; it engages everyone both internally and externally and sets the rules for doing business. It is your unique "way of being." (Insert below)*

elevating conscious branding in business

eco-aware body care

# ECOLOGÉ BRAND DNA
## (Dimensional Nucleic Assets®)

**DIFFERENTIATORS**

- 7 exclusive partnerships – with highly reputable and award-winning certified herb specialists, botanists, biologists, ecologists
- Contribute/donate to Botanical Environmental Coalition
- Importers of rare, organic-certified rainforest botanicals
- 93% of product line is all organic
- 2 proprietary production processes
- 0% synthetic or chemical ingredients
- 4 Eco-educators in our field of expertise
- 2 patented extracting processes
- Employees contribute .5% of salary towards 'enviro' causes
- Published in 13 magazines
- Use 100% recycled packaging products

**STANDARDS**

Employees:
- Hands-on Learning program, "green" philosophy – contribute

Customers:
- 100% satisfaction, "wow" personalized service w/each order; contribution to cause

Processes:
- Simple, streamlined, automated and integrated; enviro-conscious as possible

Financial:
- Ee/Cust. Incentive plans (loyalty rewards, profit pools)

**STYLE**
- Chic
- Avant Garde
- Personable
- Savvy

**VALUES**
- Environmentally Conscious
- Purity
- Simplicity
- Harmony

**Our Brand Platform/Mantra:** *your brand's fundamental essence, consistent across product categories and services. Derived from the most distinctive attributes of your DNA – usually three – four highly descriptive words.*

### Simple ~ Harmonious ~ Evolving  (SHE)

**Our Brand Promise:** *a statement that articulates your company's value proposition and exemplifies the behavioral experience you commit to deliver in every interaction, business decision, and customer touch point; it engages everyone both internally and externally and sets the rules for doing business. It is your unique "way of being".*

### Ecologé commits to enhancing personal harmony through simple environmentally conscious sensory activation of the mind, body and spirit to perpetuate evolution.

**Example:** Only (brand name) delivers, assures, guarantees.... etc. (benefit) in (product and/or service- specify) – OR – (Brand name) is the (trusted/quality/innovative) leader/provider/source (benefit) in (product and/or service - specify).

Together, your competencies, standards, style and values along with your Brand Platform and Promise build a relevant, consistent and distinctive brand experience in your customers' minds. It is your Brand DNA (Dimensional Nucleic Assets™) that distinguish you from all others in your category of products and services.

# CHAPTER 4 EXERCISE

## *Reassess Your Marketing Message*

This exercise is designed to help you reassess your marketing message and behaviors to support it based on your unique Brand DNA, Platform, and Promise. You will find Ecologé team's outputs within this exercise.

### TIME TO ALLOT:
*Allow 45 minutes–1 hour. (Schedule an official appointment in your calendar with your team, and get commitments to attend the meeting.)*

### PROPS:
*Flip chart, markers*

### WHO TO INCLUDE:
*Team of three to seven are preferred; from different areas of the business (e.g., customer service, administration, sales, etc.). If you are a start-up business or you have no employees, rally your trusted advisors, colleagues, business associates, friends, and family to assist you in generating ideas for this exercise.*

### INSTRUCTIONS
Take a look at your most recent marketing message/campaign. Review the text closely and dissect it (print ad, electronic newsletter, Web site, etc.).

1.  Use the space below to write out the brand's promise you created in chapter 3. What are the "operative" terms used to express your promise?

    a.  Brand Promise:

_____

_____

_____

_____

*Ecologé Example:*
*Ecologé commits to enhancing personal harmony through*
*sensory activation of the mind, body, and spirit.*

b.  Key terms from the promise:

i.  _____

ii.  _____

iii.  _____

*Ecologé Example:*

- *Personal harmony*
- *Sensory activation*
- *Mind, body, spirit*

2.  Does your *current* ad campaign or marketing message support your new brand promise?

If yes, how?

_____

_____

_____

If not, why not?

_____

_____

_____

*Ecologé Example:*
***We haven't leveraged the harmony through sensory activation but will now integrate this critical element into all our messaging.***

3. How will you exemplify and confirm your brand's promise through your business behaviors. When your customer is attracted by the advertisement and is compelled to make a purchase, what will create the "Wow" experience?

_____

_____

_____

*Ecologé Example:*
***We now have to "walk the talk" through the knowledge of our staff by educating our customers at every key touch point/ contact.***

4. Do you know how your competition is showing up in advertisements? Do you have samples of their ads? Is your marketing message distinctive? If so, how? (e.g. if you took the logo and company contact info off the ad, could your competitors express the same message and live up to it?)

_____

_____

_____

*Ecologé Example:*
***We have an edge with our processes, our partners, and the knowledge and personalized service of our staff. We have mystery-shopped and found that we have a huge opportunity to differentiate ourselves behaviorally.***

5. How are you *behaviorally* showing up congruent to this marketing message?

a. What systems and processes do you have in place (or need to create) to assure that your business behaviors (i.e., customer service) are congruent with your marketing message?

   i. Start by defining one behavioral process, in the area of your employees, that would be congruent to one of your style attributes.

   _____

   _____

   _____

   _____

   *Ecologé Example:*
   - *Style attribute: Savvy*
   - *Behavioral process: Ensure that all employees are educated on our processes and products so they can respond with confidence and exuberance to our customers with a minimum number of hours of product and process training.*

   ii. Start by defining one process, in the area of your employees that is congruent to one of your identified values.

   _____

   _____

   _____

   *Ecologé Example:*
   - *Value: Harmony*
   - *Behavioral process: Ensure that all employees have access to free samples and personal/family use of our products at cost; provide a mind, body, spirit room at the company office for relaxation.*

## MEG'S BREAKTHROUGH

*Dear Suzanne and Carol,*

*This time, our entire team wanted to collectively write our "breakthrough" report to you both. We are extremely excited and moved by our evolution and complete philosophical transformation since we met the Brand Ascension Group! Understanding our internal Brand DNA is creating such clarity throughout our operations and with whomever we choose to do business with. We now "get" the Universal Law of Attraction. Because we are focused on knowing who we are, great things are being generated with little effort!*

*Our new corporate identity—Wow! It is so congruent with our Brand DNA and feels very confirming. It is a constant reminder to us as to how we need to behaviorally support it!*

*We understand that the partners we choose to align ourselves with have to understand and emulate our brand philosophies. What a pleasure it is working with like-minded individuals and partnering vendors!*

*The call center partnership released all sorts of time for our reps to do what they were trained to do in building the business and nurturing our customers. We have since increased our transactions 28 percent over the last month!*

*And it is with sincere gratitude and a resounding "hip hip hooray!" for you both ... please enjoy our gift basket of assorted organic products and wine varietals as our complete appreciation for your noble and enduring brand-building services to the Ecologé team!!*

*Yours in full gratitude,*
*The Ecologé Team!*

# Chapter 5 Exercise

## *Document and Reaffirm Your Brand's Magic Story and Conduct a Touch-Point Audit*

This exercise is divided into two parts. Part A involves crafting your brand's magic story. This can be used on your Web site, in collateral, and in other literature. Part B involves conducting a touch-point audit so you can improve the customer experience at key touch points based on your Brand DNA. You will find Ecologé team's outputs within each part.

**TIME TO ALLOT:**
*Allow 30–45 minutes for part A and 30–45 for part B.*
*(Schedule an official appointment in your calendar with*
*your team, and get commitments to attend the meeting.)*
**PROPS:** *Flip chart, markers*
**WHO TO INCLUDE:**
*Team of three to seven are preferred; from different areas*
*of the business (e.g., customer service, administration,*
*sales, etc.). If you are a start-up business or you have*
*no employees, rally your trusted advisors, colleagues,*
*business associates, friends, and family to assist*
*you in generating ideas for this exercise.*

## INSTRUCTIONS

### Part A: Creating your Brand's Magic Story

Your Magic Story is a composition that includes a compelling narration of how your business and its products, services, and philosophy came to fruition. More often than not there are incredible "behind the scenes" stories that express the emotional flavor and wonder of the brand and integrity that are distinctive and interesting to your marketplace. When potential customers begin to understand in detail the depth of motivation, thought, care, quality, product-manufacturing process, etc., you will begin to carve out your specific targeted audience who greatly appreciates the value-add they receive from your brand.

We challenge you (and invite you to include your team in a brainstorming session!) to make a substantial effort in creating your brand's Magic Story. It is not only a powerful marketing tool but is an internal exercise that will continue to assist in your (and your team's) affirmation of and living of the brand they work for. It is a powerful experiential initiative that helps the brand become more solid and opens doors for new and exciting "ways of being" that just may become "rituals" for your team and culture. It is a transformative process that clarifies the perception of the brand and can possibly reengage your already loyal customers to become even more powerful brand champions (built-in sales/referral source)!

Here is a quick outline to follow, but feel free to get creative.

1. **Definition of our business brand:** *(e.g., Ecologé: an extraordinary line of pure botanical products that enhance appearance, healing, relaxation, and overall joy to be living in your skin)*

_____

_____

_____

_____

2. **Who we are:** *(e.g., We are team of ecological pioneers and eco-educators committed to enhancing our customers' mind, body, and spirit.)*

_____

_____

_____

_____

3. **How our product/service is made/delivered:** get emotional, use a lot of relevant adjectives, but be articulate *(e.g., Ecologé: from the farthest reaching Amazon rain forests to the most exotic natural botanical gardens – we work with botanists, ecologists, biologists and the like to create the finest products that nurture mind, body, and spirit.)*

---------------------------------------------------

---------------------------------------------------

---------------------------------------------------

---------------------------------------------------

4. **Our clients benefit from:** *(e.g. Ecologé: In this ever-increasing environment of overwhelming stress and stimulation, we are dedicated to bring extraordinary products to our clients at a value that is unmatched in our industry).*

---------------------------------------------------

---------------------------------------------------

---------------------------------------------------

---------------------------------------------------

## MAGIC STORY OUTLINE: (constantly refer to your specific DNA!)

### *The ECOLOGÉ MAGIC STORY—first draft*
### Definition of the business brand:

*Ecologé: An extraordinary line of harmonious, pure botanical, and natural products specifically designed to enhance the body's appearance, healing, relaxation, and your overall joy of living in your skin!*

### Who we are:

*We are a motivated, curious, and adventurous team of ecological thought leaders whose philosophy is embodied in the knowledge that Mother Earth is an amazing, complex, self-sustaining entity who provides its ecosystem with EVERYTHING necessary to thrive and evolve.*

*We sustain her efforts by supporting the research that continues to uncover her many gifts and incorporating them into the "vehicles" that create awareness and use for all who desire to know and benefit. We explore the thickest forests, the highest elevations, the deepest oceans, the most pure valleys to discover her infinite "magic" potions for living life with ultimate comfort and experiential pleasure.*

### How our product/service is made/delivered:

*From the farthest-reaching Amazon rain forests to the most exotic natural botanical gardens, we work with botanists, ecologists, biologists, and the like to compose 100 percent natural compounds that add to and accentuate our customer's lifestyles. We bring these products to you free of synthetic chemicals and known allergens via our virtual storefront and through carefully selected partner alliances that share our philosophies and passions.*

*Our delivery is swift and streamlined so that you receive your order within two days, carefully and elegantly contained in enviro-friendly packaging, ready for you to fully experience. All of our customers receive up to three samples of our extended product lines based on their presubmitted client profile. We like to surprise our patrons with special incentives, value packages, and bonus gifts with every order!*

### Our clients benefit from:

*In our ever-increasing environment of stress, multitasking, and toxins, we believe that the last thing your body needs is more synthetics of unknown origins to sift through and sort out that cause potential damage. Our clients benefit from what Mother Earth has so wittingly provided our inhabitants to use, reuse, and flourish in her bounty. With the use of our oils, lotions, bath salts, shampoos, fragrances, and teas, our clients are nurtured by soothing, healing, and rejuvenating products in so many ways. When we allow ourselves to stop, relax, and relish in nature, our authentic self rises to the surface and abundance abounds!*

## Part B: Conducting a Touch-Point Audit

Let's take a moment to discover and outline all the instances where your business touches your customers/clients. Put yourself in their shoes for a moment and sift through all the various areas the business exposes itself to you as the customer via your products, services, and relationships. Take this touch-point audit and list the instances (e.g., referrals, on-site visits, online, e-newsletter, product education, invoicing, follow-up, coupons, business cards, direct-mail, etc.).

1. Touch-point instance:

    _____

    _____

    _____

    a) How is the above instance currently delivered? (Briefly describe the play-by-play process.)

        _____

        _____

        _____

    b) How can you enhance the touch-point delivery: (e.g., if one of your values is relationships and one of our styles is fun, then what specific behavior can be created to reflect these two attributes within that touch point? (refer to DNA)

        i) Attribute: _____

            behavior looks like: _____

        ii) Attribute: _____

            behavior looks like: _____

        Revised instance of delivery looks like this: (description of the new touch-point protocol):

        _____

        _____

        _____

        _____

## *Ecologé Example of a Touch-point Audit*

***Touch-Point Instance (B2B):*** *First Contact with Potential Partner/ Vendor*

1. ***How contact is currently delivered:*** *Currently a professional letter is written on our stationery to the identified contact/buyer of product. The letter introduces Ecologé, our product line, and our pricing structure. We then follow up with a phone call to secure a face-to-face meeting or conference call.*

2. ***How can we enhance the touch-point delivery:*** *Based on your DNA, what specific behavior can you create to reflect these two attributes within that touch point?*

   a) ***Attribute:*** *Enviro-Consciousness (value)* **...** ***behavior looks like:*** *Make sure that our corporate logo/stationery paper is on our "recycled" paper. Include professionally designed flyer of research results with the benefits and powerful characteristics of natural botanical products. This should include pictures of the Ecologé team in botanist labs (our partners) where the natural ingredients are tested.*

   b) ***Attribute:*** *Personable and Chic (style)* **...** ***behavior looks like:*** *Create a mock "profile" page of partner/vendor with key personality points of the vendor company and justifications for them to be included on one of the specially selected "VIP" list of chosen partner/vendors for Ecologé products. (We will perform some research on each partner/vendor and incorporate this into the profile page to indicate to them that we know who they are.) We'll also add several samples of Ecologé products wrapped in enviro-friendly ribbon attaching handwritten gift tags with the personalized name of the contact. Each sample will have a brief but highly articulate description of the benefits, ingredients, and special differentiators.*

3. ***Revised instance of delivery looks like this:*** *(description of the new touch-point protocol):*

   a) *Research partner vendor to fulfill layout of "Profile Page" (name, company, position, company philosophies, locations, market profile, etc.; kind of like an FBI profile page—with their company logo).*

   b) *Select three sample items to personalize for the prospect to experience.*

    c)   *Specialty wrap and label with handwritten name on card attached to sample.*

    d)   *Complete introduction letter on Ecologé stationery, sign, and attach business card. Roll letter into tube—tie with ribbon.*

    e)   *Place samples, specially scented potpourri sash, profile, and intro letter in special two-foot enviro-friendly sturdy paper tube with "Special delivery" label. Send via priority mail.*

## MEG'S LATEST COMMENTS

*Dear Carol and Suzanne:*

*I cannot believe it—you did it again! Completing this exercise exceeded my expectations! I love getting my team involved in "operationalizing" my brand. They are so excited at our meetings and continue to come up with ideas, even when they are not at work! I have gotten several calls from my key people telling me they just had a "BFO!" (blinding flash of the obvious) of how we can start doing this or that. The creativity is amazing—I even catch them doing "brand checks" to make sure that we are staying congruent with our DNA. The first package we sent out to our partner/vendor was a huge success! They couldn't wait for us to call them; they phoned us the afternoon they received the package. We are finalizing our order/delivery with them at the end of the week. This is becoming so fun!*

*Hats off again to both of you!*

*Meg*
*CEO, Chief Strategist*
*Ecologé Botanical Products*
*www.BodyEcologé.com*

# CHAPTER 6 EXERCISE

## *Assess and Align Your Brand Behaviors to Your Values and Style Attributes*

Remember that building an authentic and successful brand is about consistently showing up the way you say you are—your unique Brand DNA. There are two parts to this exercise. In part A you will assess how consistent you are as brand in living your values and style attributes. In part B you will identify those with the biggest gaps in consistency and develop actions to address the gaps. You will find Ecologé team's outputs within each part.

**TIME TO ALLOT:**
*Allow 25–30 minutes for part A and 45–60 minutes for part B. (Schedule an official appointment in your calendar with your team, and get commitments to attend the meeting.)*
**PROPS:**
*Flip chart, markers*
**WHO TO INCLUDE:**
*Team of three to seven are preferred; from different areas of the business (e.g., customer service, administration, sales, etc.). If you are a start-up business or you have no employees, rally your trusted advisors, colleagues, business associates, friends, and family to assist you in generating ideas for this exercise.*

## INSTRUCTIONS

### Part A:

In exercise 1, we discussed that when a business is in alignment to what it stands for, it shows up more authentic and consistent. This alignment occurs when your values and style attributes are consistent with your behaviors. We referred to this consistency as "Cognitive Resonance." When the behaviors don't match, there is inconsistency. We call this "Cognitive Dissonance." These inconsistent actions create the potential for mistrust with your employees and customers.

1. Look at your values and style attributes and assess how well you are living up to them. Please refer to the definitions you created for each in chapter 1. We find that all businesses find opportunities or gaps for improvement.
2. List each of your core values and style attributes in the left column below. In the right column, rate how consistent you are in living each value and style attribute.

| **Value** | **Consistency in Living Our Value** |
|---|---|
| | 1=Never, 2=Occasionally, 3=Frequently, 4=Almost Always, 5=Always |
| _____ | _____ |
| _____ | _____ |
| _____ | _____ |
| _____ | _____ |
| _____ | _____ |

| **Style Attribute** | **Consistency in Living Our Style** |
|---|---|
| | 1=Never, 2=Occasionally, 3=Frequently, 4=Almost Always, 5=Always |
| _____ | _____ |
| _____ | _____ |
| _____ | _____ |

_____     _____

_____     _____

### *Ecologé Example:*

| **Value** | **Consistency in Living Our Value**<br>1=Never, 2=Occasionally, 3=Frequently, 4=Almost Always, 5=Always |
|---|---|
| *Environmentally Conscious* | *3* |
| *Purity* | *5* |
| *Simplicity* | *4* |
| *Harmony* | *4* |

| **Style Attribute** | **Consistency in Living Our Style**<br>1=Never, 2=Occasionally, 3=Frequently, 4=Almost Always, 5=Always |
|---|---|
| *Chic* | *3* |
| *Avant-garde* | *5* |
| *Personable* | *4* |
| *Savvy* | *4* |

## Part B:

Now here is the first step to creating alignment and gaining the trust needed for your customers to be loyal to your brand!

- *Hint:* Try getting several of your employees or trusted advisors to do this exercise individually; then come together to discuss your collective results. No doubt you will have some interesting points of view. Then collaborate and agree as a group.

Select from each category (value and style) those with the biggest gap. Identify at least one or two behaviors or actions you will take and introduce into your organization to close the gap and the timing for each.

**Value:** _____

**ACTIONS:**                    **TIMING:**

_____        _____

_____        _____

_____        _____

_____        _____

_____        _____


**Style Attribute:** _____

**ACTIONS:**                    **TIMING:**

_____        _____

_____        _____

_____        _____

_____        _____

_____        _____


*Ecologé Example:*
*Value: Environmentally conscious*

*ACTIONS and (Timing):*
1. *Source appropriate vendor so that our packaging consists of 100 percent recycled materials (currently about 85–90 percent recycled materials). (Within 1–2 months)*
2. *Update all our packaging with 100 percent recycled materials. (Within 6 months)*

*Style Attribute: Chic*

*ACTIONS and (Timing):*
1. *Revamp Web site; needs to be greatly improved relative to the look, feel, and navigation so as to be more visually congruent with the definition of our chic style. (Within 3–4 months)*

2. *Marketing collateral needs to be updated to be more consistent with our chic style. (Update design and reprint within 6 months.) Note: will also ensure the changes above reflect our other value attributes: avant-garde, personable, and savvy*

You're on a roll now—don't stop!! Building your brand is right around the corner!

## MEG'S BREAKTHROUGH

*Hello Brand Ascension!*

*Ecologé is ascending nicely with the last exercise! Wow! Not to say it was easy, but it required that we get super serious about how we exemplify our brand in every area of the business! What an eye opener!*

*My team is becoming more and more tuned in, not only with the business, but as a real team! They are conversing with one another more than ever and sharing ideas on improvements and new ways to improve how we show up as a brand. They are even coming up with some significant goals for other changes, such as enhancements to our service to excel in our personable and savvy style attributes and how to better educate our customers on what makes us so unique and why they should continue to do business with us! I never realized how this exercise would create such synergy among us!*

*I cannot wait until we review this with you—I can feel how our brand is becoming its own powerful entity that we are all working toward and also wanting to protect and manage. I sense a much greater "ownership" from my team! I cannot thank you enough!*

*Are we still on for next Tuesday at 9:00 am? You are going to be so proud! ☺ Have a great weekend!*

*Meg*
*CEO, Chief Strategist*
*Ecologé Botanical Products*
*www.BodyEcologé.com*

# Chapter 7 Exercise

## *Define Your Ideal Customer*

This exercise is designed to help you define your ideal customer. You will find Ecologé team's outputs within this exercise.

**TIME TO ALLOT:**
*Allow 45 minutes–1 hour. (Schedule an official appointment in your calendar with your team, and get commitments to attend the meeting.)*

**PROPS:**
*Flip chart, markers*

**WHO TO INCLUDE:**
*Team of three to seven are preferred; from different areas of the business (e.g., customer service, administration, sales, etc.). If you are a start-up business or you have no employees, rally your trusted advisors, colleagues, business associates, friends, and family to assist you in generating ideas for this exercise.*

## INSTRUCTIONS

Now is the time to take the reins and define your ideal customer as a reflection of what your business stands for. Once you are absolutely clear on your ideal customer it is easier to attract them to you. But you must first define what your ideal customer is.

Take the values and style attributes you completed in exercise 1 and your Brand Platform in exercise 3. If you have not finished these exercises, then take the time to do so right now. Don't delay, because you won't be able to move on without this completed. If you have completed the exercise, then congratulations for sticking to the task as you are well on your way to elevating your brand.

Now take your brand's style attributes, values, and Brand Platform and begin to define your target customer (refer to the example directly following this exercise). Be sure to review your definitions of the values and style attributes you completed in exercise 1. (See Ecologé example following this exercise.)

**Our Values**                                    **Our Style Attributes**

_____              _____

_____              _____

_____              _____

_____              _____

_____              _____

**Our Brand Platform**

_____

Now begin to define your ideal customer in the following section based on the descriptive qualities of your values and style attributes (see Ecologé example at end of this exercise).

**Our Ideal Customer:**

1. _____

   _____

   _____

   _____

2. _____

   _____

   _____

   _____

3. _____

_____

_____

_____

4. _____

_____

_____

_____

Notes:




The Brand DNA process is the first critical step in clearly articulating your brand so you can serve as a mirror reflection of the customers you desire to serve.

### *Ecologé Example*

**Values Definitions**
- **Environmentally conscious:** *Conduct business with a "green" philosophy by educating ourselves and our customers on the importance of using only biodegradable products (ingredients and packaging).*
- **Purity:** *Offer only certified organic and natural products of the highest-quality elements of nature: herbs and flower essences, essential oils, natural sea salts, etc.*
- **Simplicity:** *Minimalist packaging and containers to preserve the delicate balance of all ingredients and serving as a natural expression of their essence.*
- **Harmony:** *Act in concert with nature by preserving the natural balance of mind, body, and spirit.*

**Style Attribute Definitions**

- **Chic:** *Simple elegance to reflect a refined and stylish yet minimalist look and feel to how we visually show up in our packaging, on our Web site, in our marketing collateral, and in personal dress in representing the brand.*
- **Avant-garde:** *In pursuit of distinguishing characteristics that reflect unconventional and progressive attitudes. We intend to "push the envelope" in thought, form, and substance.*
- **Personable:** *Warm and engaging behaviors that reflect the friendly and approachable nature of all our associates in our interactions with one another, our customers, and the communities we serve.*
- **Savvy:** *Confident, well-informed, and knowledgeable; our products and research will ensure that customers receive the finest botanicals and elements of nature.*

**BRAND PLATFORM:**

Simple - Harmonious - Evolving (SHE)

**Simple:** uncomplicated, pure

**Harmonious:** complementary and balanced

**Evolving:** constant state of change for the better

Notice below how the Ecologé team focused on specific categories and defined the mindset for each. They got highly focused on defining their ideal customer by how they share Ecologé's values, style, and Brand Platform. To attract customers who fit your brand you need to be highly tuned in to the characteristics of your market.

**Ecologé Ideal Client Is:**

*A progressive thinker who is proactive and socially responsible; self-directed while seeking to continually understand, grow, and prosper; ecologically wise; more concerned with environmental sustainability and the most efficient and effective production, purchase, use, and disposal of products and how we source from the earth—its effect on our lives, the environment, and generations to come; willing to pay more to ensure a balance by living in harmony with nature rather than trying to control nature; desiring of a simpler and lower-stress lifestyle; willing to take every opportunity to nurture mind, body, and spirit for self and others.*

**Individuals** *who have an appreciation of and are seeking balance and healing through the purchase and use of pure, eco-friendly body-care products and therapies that are in harmony with nature; who have a strong desire to promote a "green philosophy" to others. They appreciate learning about new products and being educated on eco-friendly practices.*

**Entrepreneurs and business owners** *who are knowledgeable and have a passion for educating, promoting, and selling the highest-quality natural organic body-care products to the general consumer, associates, and their communities. These businesses are progressive in their business practices. They insist on being knowledgeable and confident in the products they sell. They stand behind a 100 percent satisfaction guarantee. They also appreciate a friendly and personal touch to doing business.*

**Organizations (e.g., resorts and spas, hotels, etc.)** *across the globe specializing in educating and providing natural body-care products and therapies of a "green philosophy" to their guests to enable the restoring balance of mind, body, and spirit. Enjoy a friendly, personable touch to doing business. Stand behind a 100 percent satisfaction guarantee.*

## MEG' S BREAKTHROUGH

Meg was astounded at the process we provided to her and within a week came back to us with the following note via e-mail:

> *Dear Carol and Suzanne,*
>
> *Incredible! I can't thank you enough for the process you had us work through to define my ideal target customer. I am absolutely delighted to have pushed through this exercise. I worked with two of my team members on this exercise, and here's what we came up for our ideal customer based on our style, values, and Brand Platform. (Please see the attached Word document.)*
>
> *I feel so much more confident now than before. Just to let you know, I did go back to the resort and spa prospect and told him that we did not feel we were a good fit for his needs given the philosophy upon which Ecologé was founded and that we have decided to withdraw our proposal. There was dead silence at the other end of the line. I think they were in shock. We politely parted ways.*

*The next day we received a phone call from another resort spa company we are pursuing for a substantial contract. Everything we have done thus far supports and reaffirms that this new prospect is our ideal client. It is the perfect match in the hotel and resort arena. The company meets our criteria of the ideal client and is very excited to meet with us. This is meant to be. My team and I feel it. By letting go of the other prospect, we then allowed room to attract this new, more appropriate prospect. We are so energized to close this sale. Stay tuned!*

*I am now clearer and focused on who we need to attract as customers to the Ecologé brand and am working on developing a strategy for attracting and acquiring the right customers, which I'd like to review with you soon.*

*Thank you from the bottom of my heart for your insights and advice.*

*Warmly,*
*Meg*
*CEO, Chief Strategist*
*Ecologé Botanical Products*
*www.BodyEcologé.com*

# CHAPTER 8 EXERCISE

## *Leverage the Power of the Senses to Build Your Brand Experience*

This exercise has two parts. Part A consists of brainstorming the application of the senses to reaffirm your Brand DNA, Platform, and Promise. Part B consists of identifying actions to build a branded sensory experience through the ideas you generated in part A. You will find Écologé team's outputs within each part.

**TIME TO ALLOT:**

*Allow 25–30 minutes for part A and 45–60
minutes for part B. (Schedule an official
appointment in your calendar with your team,
and get commitments to attend the meeting.)*

**PROPS:**

*Flip chart, markers*

**WHO TO INCLUDE:**

*Team of three to seven are preferred; from different areas
of the business (e.g., customer service, administration,
sales, etc.). If you are a start-up business or you have
no employees, rally your trusted advisors, colleagues,
business associates, friends, and family to assist
you in generating ideas for this exercise.*

Let's capitalize on the power of understanding and leverage the human senses. Remember that the more sensory memories that are activated with the customer/client the greater the bond is to the product or service. So the question becomes, how can your brand become more experiential through the senses? This activity will assist you and your team in discovering ways to enhance the sensory memories of your customers and be congruent with your Brand DNA. Have fun with this and get creative!

## INSTRUCTIONS

Bring together a few of your team members, or if you are a solopreneur, bring together those you trust and know what your brand is all about, and brainstorm the following exercise. You'll be amazed at how creative you can be.

***Note:*** Feel free to refer to the sensory exercise completed by Meg and her team at Ecologé, which follows the exercise template (Exhibit 3) on page 178.

## Part A: Applying Your Brand DNA, Brand Platform, and Promise through the Senses

Here's where you really begin to "show up" with your unique brand. By following these guidelines consciously and consistently, you can establish a solid, powerful brand foundation and set the rules for engagement with everyone you come in contact and interact with. Start with answering the questions below. Decide on ways to match your brand DNA to the sensory perceptions people use to formulate consistent, relevant, and distinctive impressions of you. (If you downloaded the workbook in PDF you will find a full-size copy to use in completing this exercise.)

There are no right or wrong answers; only those that accurately represent who you are! So ask yourself, "How does my brand essence/promise appeal to the following senses?" And fill in the blanks below to begin this sensory journey. Make copies of this or use another sheet to continue brainstorming ideas with your teams.

# Exhibit 3

## *Applying Your Brand DNA Through the Senses*

Here's where you really begin to 'show up'! By following these guidelines consciously and consistently, you begin establishing a solid, powerful brand foundation - and setting the rules for engagement with everyone you come in contact and interact with. Begin by deciding on ways to match your Brand DNA to the sensory perceptions your customers/employees use to help them formulate consistent, relevant, and distinctive impressions of your brand. There are NO right or wrong answers, only those that accurately represent who you are! So ask yourself "how does my brand appeal to the following senses?" and fill out the blanks below.

## SENSE: | EXPERIENCE:

 What does my Brand DNA **LOOK** like? Consider your physical attributes; how you and your team look, dress, your approach/demeanor; consistency in color schemes and office environment, your business collateral, business cards, etc.

_____

 What does my Brand DNA **SOUND** like? Consider your personal brand speak (vocabulary) distinctive tone or pitch. If your brand reflected a specific genre of music, what would that be? What does your office environment 'sound' like? What is the tone of your voice message?

_____

 What does my Brand DNA **SMELL** like? Consider what particular scent resonates with your brand that you want others to associate with you. Smell is the most powerful memory enhancing sense your customers have.

_____

 What does my Brand DNA **TASTE** like? Consider what tastes you want others to associate or experience with you; specialty coffee, water, tea, wine, energy drinks? If your brand were a flavor, what would it be? Do you give corporate gifts? Referral gifts? Consider adding a 'flavor' to your gift-giving.

_____

 What are my Brand DNA **TOUCH** qualities? Consider what textures of clothing or fabric on office furniture are representative of the brand; how you shake your customer's hand. Does your environment feel soft and comfortable or have more of an industrial feel? Consider the feel of your proposals, your business cards, etc.

_____

 What does my brand **EXPRESS INTUITIVELY**? Consider how your entire brand experience makes people feel as they interact with you, your products and services. What is the overall impression left with the customer? How can you enhance that?

_____

*Ecologé Example:*

## SENSORY EXERCISE

**What does my brand DNA LOOK like?** *Our offices and new retail outlet (when open) reflect the blue and green hues of our brand trade identity with its softness and simple flowing lines. Our furniture and décor reflects this simple timelessness and relaxing feel to our look. Our walls are accented with cool blue and refreshing green—colors matching our logo. Our green and blue tiled floor will deepen and authenticate our visual presence with subtle directional pathways to the different areas of the retail store and offices.*

**What does my brand DNA SOUND like?** *We have relaxing, ethereal-like/quality sounds—no lyrics; just ethereal music of soft chimes as they rustle in the wind. Several waterfall and fountain fixtures emit sounds of gentle flowing water, a bubbling brook, etc., all synergistically combined to take us to a relaxed, balanced state that depicts the merging of mind, body, and spirit.*

**What does my brand DNA SMELL like?** *Soothing essences of lavender, myrrh, frankincense, chamomile, sage, and the like. Our employees wear these essences. Essential oils and aromatherapy infuse a fresh, clean, and invigorating scent through the air of our offices and future retail outlets, creating a calming effect. We offer free samples to our customers.*

**What does my brand DNA TASTE like?** *Hints of vanilla and soft apricot, peach and pear notes. We stock healthy snacks of pure, natural, and organic ingredients through a partner alliance in our break room, in our retail outlets, and as gifts to customers. A light and crisp chardonnay with buttery notes … pure and simple for company events, client anniversaries, holidays, and other special occasion gifts of choice.*

**What does my brand DNA FEEL LIKE TACTILELY?** *Our seating is delicate in form and ergonomically correct, relieving any back or posture symptoms* *with kapok-filled hemp-fabric pillows nestled in overstuffed lamb leather chairs, inviting clients and employees to succumb to comfort and relaxation.*

**What does my brand DNA EXPRESS INTUITIVELY?** *Our employees and customers want to linger and take in the essence of the soothing moments of relaxing mind, body, and spirit. No rush ... there is a calm and balanced feeling of mind, body, and spirit. The smell, the feel, the visual and auditory stimulus invite the customer to slow down and enjoy.*

Now based on the sensory ideas you formulated complete part B.

## Part B: Enhancing Your Brand Experience through the Senses

Let's create two memorable actions/behaviors by applying at least two or more of the senses: (Feel free to refer to the sensory ideas for memorable events completed by Meg and her team at Ecologé at the end of this exercise.)

- One **INTERNAL** *(for your employees—example: typical day on the job, orientation, employee birthday, etc.) and*
- One **EXTERNAL** *(for your customers—example: presenting a proposal to a potential buyer, servicing an existing customer, etc.)*

1. **INTERNAL MEMORABLE ACTION/BEHAVIOR (Employees):**

---

---

**SENSES ACTIVATED:** Identify two or more.

---

---

Describe in the space below …

_____

_____

_____

_____

_____

_____

## 2. EXTERNAL MEMORABLE ACTION/BEHAVIOR (Customers):

_____

_____

**SENSES ACTIVATED:** Identify two or more.

_____

_____

Describe in the space below …

_____

_____

_____

_____

_____

_____

_____

*Ecologé Example:*

**INTERNAL MEMORABLE EVENT: Employee's typical day on the job.
(SENSES ACTIVATED: Sight, Sound, Smell, Taste, Touch,
Intuition)**

*We have transformed a small, intimate area in our offices (and planned for our retail outlets) into a space fully dedicated to relaxation—an internal sanctuary of sort. It includes a library of resources on eco-studies. Every employee has the opportunity to take a break to relieve stress and tension and enjoy its rejuvenating benefits. This sanctuary is filled with aromatherapy oils and samples of all our products. There is a massage chair along with complimentary and calming refreshments of water and assorted organic teas and wholesome light snacks. Soft, ethereal music plays continuously in the background to elicit a relaxed state of mind—all reflecting the essence of the Ecologé Brand Platform to enhance balance of mind, body, and spirit.*

**EXTERNAL MEMORABLE EVENT: Distribution of our monthly
catalog of products to customers
(SENSES ACTIVATED: Sight, Sound, Smell, Touch, Intuition)**

*Every customer receives a monthly catalog with a complimentary sample of our featured product. The catalog is printed on special recycled paper with a distinctive look and feel, reflecting the simplicity and purity of the Ecologé brand. We enclose an updated educational piece on research around environmentally safe use of our products. Twice a year, we enclose a special, value-added bonus: a complimentary CD with a collection of our favorite music and a representation of the true essence of our brand. In each order delivery, we enclose an Ecologé Enviro-Conscious Card™.*

## MEG'S BREAKTHROUGH

*Dear Suzanne and Carol,*

*Well, once again, I can't thank you enough for the encouragement, consultation, and prodding to dig deep into how to create simple yet congruent experiences among my team and our customers. We have brainstormed some phenomenal sensory ideas that I never would have thought about doing. We have already begun the steps to implement a few of these ideas among ourselves and our customers and have seen an increase in new referrals of over 37 percent.*

*Hope you don't mind that we decided to run with it. We are excited to push forward. Can't wait to share further news as we progress along this wonderful journey of brand elevation for Ecologé.*

*Sincerely,*
*Meg* ☺☺☺
*CEO, Chief Strategist*
*Ecologé Botanical Products*
*www.BodyEcologé.com*

# EPILOGUE

Ecologé is off to an amazing journey in the evolution of its brand. Meg and her team have built their Brand DNA foundation and have created the road map that will endure for the life of the brand. The company continues to evolve the Ecologé differentiators and standards of its brand to stay innovative and ahead of the competition. The brand's style and value attributes remain true and as apparent as ever in Meg and her team's relevant and distinctive actions and behaviors. She has carved out a notable, memorable, and consistent brand that has earned her much notoriety and industry respect.

After two years of integrating the Brand DNA into every fabric of its organization, Ecologé is receiving numerous accolades from its customers, who are avid brand champions. 75 percent of their customers buy from them on a regular basis. Prior to the Brand DNA process, Ecologé was struggling to build and sustain a loyal following. Their customers report that they love the company's products and appreciate the level of personalized service provided. Recently, Meg and her team created an advisory council consisting of several key customers. They confer with this special advisory council to solicit ideas for new products and ways to enhance their services. In fact, 99 percent of new product ideas come from customers. Not many brands can claim this kind of success.

Meg is now speaking more frequently not only to her industry but to organizations that cater to business building practices. She recently won a regional small business of the year award from her industry and is capitalizing on creating even more buzz about her brand-building techniques through the use of social media in blogs, on Twitter, Facebook, and in her LinkedIn professional profile. Meg is now an official member of the Brand Ascension Group's Brand Ascension Institute Affiliate Member program (you can become a member too! www.BrandAscension.com). She regularly sends us referrals of great, visionary entrepreneurs that have the drive and motivation to be the best in their industry.

# Afterword

After defining your brand, building a brand is truly all about being hyperconscious of what your brand represents in every facet of your organization. We acknowledge how time-consuming building a business is just in the details of the business itself, let alone adding a "personality" or set of brand "standards" to the mix. However, these are the pieces to the puzzle that helps your brand create uniqueness, consistency, and true relevancy within your market.

We'd also like to add in the element of emotion as a powerful contributor to brand success. Building your brand's unique DNA helps you connect specific emotional elements to your business, its employees, and very importantly, your customers. Too many times businesses have started and failed because they missed this key emotional connection.

We believe that starting and running a business should be fun, challenging, creative, and profitable! When you undertake this step-by-step brand-defining and brand-building process you reach a new level of intimacy with your business, which creates a paradigm shift in how your business is received by your market space. Not only you, as the owner, but your employee team have a deeper level of commitment and "brand buy-in" as they begin to better understand their contribution to the brand and their role in expressing it.

Remember that branding is a process, not an event, and that this level of consciousness around your brand should continue for the life of your organization, not just by you, the owner, but by all its stakeholders. Clearly articulating your Brand DNA will help streamline many other facets of the business (e.g., marketing, communications, employee hiring, partnering, business decisions, etc.). When you achieve this level, you will see your business thrive!

# ABOUT THE AUTHORS

**Carol Chapman** and **Suzanne Tulien** are principals and cofounders of the Brand Ascension Group (BA Group), based out of Colorado Springs, CO USA. They are committed to organizations that want to achieve transformational and sustainable brand success through *strategic, internal branding* practices. As co-developers of pioneering brand elevation methodologies—Brand DNA (Dimensional Nucleic Assets®) and the Brand DNA System™—they have helped numerous small to medium-sized businesses create consistent, relevant, and distinctive experiences that engage, inspire, and win their employees and customers for life.

As engaging speakers and certified trainers in experiential and accelerated adult-learning methodologies, BA Group delivers highly effective keynotes, brand consulting and facilitation onsite, online (virtual Web-based), and on demand that engage the different learning styles and ways humans process information: auditory, visual, kinesthetic, and intellectual. Their techniques maximize and ensure each person's contribution to the brand-building process and the overall strategic positioning of the brand as part of the organization's core business strategy.

**Carol Chapman** has held several executive management roles, including Vice President of Human Resources-Asia Pacific for the largest hotel company in the world-InterContinental Hotels Group (IHG) – formerly Six Continents Hotels and Bass Hotels & Resorts.

As an engaging international speaker and consultant, she has presented at major conferences and events in London, Singapore, Bali and the U.S – inspiring audiences. She regularly trains and presents webinars on brand culture and employee engagement, brand definition, brand strategy and management for small to medium sized businesses and is author of numerous articles.

Carol holds a Bachelor of Science Degree in Criminal Justice/Human Behavior from Georgia State University. She also holds the following certifications: Certified Executive Coach, Certified in Emotional Intelligence, and Certified Train-the-Trainer (Accelerated/Experiential Learning).

As a Brand Culture Creative, speaker, consultant and trainer, Carol is leading a new breed of next generation businesses to leverage the power of internal brand strategies that deliver enhanced performance and perception of their brands.

**Suzanne Tulien** has held several previous key roles. She was founder of I.D. by Design—a creative boutique specializing in corporate identity design and brand consulting. Prior to that, she served as creative project manager for a global consulting firm, Navigant Consulting. And before that, facilitated marketing training workshops across the U.S. with Jungle Marketing.

A captivating and experiential speaker and trainer, Suzanne has presented at a variety of conferences events across the U.S. She regularly presents workshops and webinars on brand culture, employee engagement, brand definition, and brand strategy for small to medium sized businesses. She regularly writes articles for newsletters and is frequently published on BrandChannel.com, Innova, eHotelier, and YoungEntrepreneur.com, to name a few.

Suzanne holds a Bachelor of Arts Degree in Organizational Communications and Graphic Design, University of South Alabama. She is an award winning graphic designer and a certified trainer (Level II) as well as certified in accelerated learning methodologies. Suzanne is also an expert panel member of YoungEntrepreneur.com.

As a Brand Culture Creative, speaker, consultant and trainer, Suzanne is guiding business brands with advocacy, intention, momentum and purpose to define, create and build compelling brand experiences from the inside out.

View their Web site at www.BrandAscension.com and sign up for their eNewsletter. Subscribe to their blog at http://brandascension.com/blog/ and contact them at info@BrandAscension.com.

Follow them on Twitter:
http://twitter.com/CarolChapman
http://twitter.com/SuzTulien
http://twitter.com/BrandAscension

# PART III
# BRANDING TOOLS
# AND RESOURCES

# BRAND TERMINOLOGY

(Glossary of Branding Terms)

**Authentic Brand:** A brand that is "true" to what it stands for—as demonstrated through employees' thoughts, actions, and interactions with one another and with customers—and that has achieved a strong emotional bond and level of trust both internally (with employees) and externally (with customers, vendors, partners, and communities).

**Brand Advantage:** The result of ensuring a favorable position in the market by continually differentiating the brand behaviorally, enhancing the brand experience, innovating, and evolving the brand.

**Brand Culture:** A unique system of shared beliefs, values, customs, and behaviors that people cultivate and emulate through learning and experience with the brand. Brand culture comes alive both internally with employees and externally with customers (e.g., the Harley Owners Group®—a membership organization of one million people around the world united by a common passion: making the Harley-Davidson® dream a way of life—www.HarleyDavidson.com).

**Brand Diagnostic:** A baseline assessment through employee and customer surveys, focus groups, etc., that captures how a brand is currently perceived both internally and externally relative to its Brand DNA—its distinctive attributes.

**Brand DNA:** A brand's Dimensional Nucleic Assets®. The genetic code for success consisting of the most distinguishing brand attributes—values, style, differentiators, and standards, brand platform, and brand promise—upon which to create competitive advantage and build an authentic brand.

**The Brand DNA System**[SM]**:** A step-by-step conscious, deliberate, and strategic process consisting of four critical phases—define, assess, build, and evolve—that ensures the elevation and sustainability of a brand over time.

**Brand Engagement:** How an organization embeds the brand in contexts that generate strong emotional responses (of a brand experience) that resonates in terms of an individual's personal needs and values.

**Brand Experience:** The feeling or sensation (positive or negative) a person has as a result of personal contact with the brand, its products and services, and its employees. Positive brand "experiences are events that engage individuals in an inherently *personal way* ... They actually occur on an emotional, physical, intellectual or even spiritual level" (taken from *The Experience Economy: Work Is Theatre & Every Business a Stage by Joseph Pine II and James Gilmore, 1999)*. "A Brand is a living entity—and it is enriched or undermined cumulatively over time, the product of a thousand small gestures" (Michael Eisner).

**Brand Management:** A proactive process that organizations take to continuously measure, monitor, and adapt behaviors and business practices to safeguard the integrity and evolution of their brand and ensure continued brand advantage.

**Brand Perception:** The sum of all impressions that consumers have for a brand based on their emotion and defined by their experience (as taken in through all the senses—sight, sound, taste, touch, smell, and intuition) with the brand, its products and services, and its employees.

**Brand Platform/Mantra:** The fundamental essence, nature, or quality of a brand. The Brand Platform is like a "mantra" and is derived from the most distinctive attributes of the Brand DNA—usually two to three highly descriptive words. It is the platform for emulating the brand's unique "way of being."

**Brand Presence:** The extent to which an organization and its employees understand the essence of what the brand stands for through "thinking and acting with full awareness" to elevate the brand in the mind of its market.

**Brand Promise:** A declaration and commitment that articulates a brand's value proposition. It exemplifies the behavioral experience the organization commits to deliver in every interaction, business decision, and customer touch point. It engages everyone both internally and externally and sets the rules for doing business.

**Brand Scorecard:** The Brand Scorecard creates a balanced perspective within the business to reinforce your Brand DNA and helps set standards and track performance in four key areas: employees, customers, processes, and financial. It is customized to your organization and is used to establish priorities and metrics that support your business/brand strategy.

**Brand Strategic Roadmap:** The "brand guidance system" consisting of highly targeted actions and strategies resulting in consistent and distinctive "on-brand" experiences. It reaffirms the brand at every touch point, allowing the ability to adapt to changing market conditions through the alignment of strategy, leadership, culture, business processes, and metrics.

**Brand Vocabulary:** Organizations use specific vocabulary as expressive means of communication that people can share with a common comprehension. Brand vocabulary is a distinctive and meaningful way to reflect the unique and distinctive attributes of a brand both internally (with employees) and externally (with customers).

**Branding:** The process of creating and living a brand's message. The process starts at the internal level with a clear understanding of what the brand stands for—its unique Brand DNA—company values and behaviors, the culture created that represents those values, customer-relationship practices, and the sensory experiences created and delivered through consistent systems and processes.

**Byline:** A descriptive phrase accompanying a brand's name that communicates the business or industry the brand is in.

**Marketing:** The process of communicating and disseminating a brand's message. It is a key part of the external brand experience through the creative vehicles used to market the business, such as advertising and promotional campaigns, signage, PR activities, a Web site, trade shows, etc.

**On-brand:** An organization that has aligned its leadership, culture, business processes and metrics to consistently deliver experiences that are highly brand-relevant to its Brand DNA.

**Tagline:** A descriptive phrase accompanying a brand's name that describes the WIIFM (what's in it for me?) to those the brand wants to attract both internally and externally.

# BRAND BEHAVIOR™ ASSESSMENT

The following questions are designed as a self-assessment to help you determine the "elevation" your brand has reached in differentiating itself behaviorally. Behaviors that are consistent with what your brand stands for are key factors in creating competitive advantage.

**Each question has the following choices**
   RATING SCALE: 1 = Never; 2 = Sometimes; 3 = Often; 4 = Always

   **Rate each statement using the above scale**                **Rating**

1.  Our employees behave in ways that reflect our distinctive personality and core values as a brand.               _____

2.  We benchmark our behaviors against leading practices of highly successful brands.               _____

3.  We hire employees based on behavioral attributes that reflect our organizational values.               _____

4.  Employees attend customer-service training/education that emphasizes acceptable standards of behavior reflective of our brand values and personality.               _____

5.  Our employees use a unique "brand vocabulary" that sets us apart behaviorally from other organizations.               _____

6.  We monitor (e.g., call monitoring, observation, etc.) specific and accepted behaviors of our employees that reflect what we stand for as a brand.               _____

7.  We ask our customers for performance feedback relative to the behaviors of our employees.               _____

8.  We review our processes to ensure that they support our employees in delivering a differentiated behavioral experience.               _____

9.  Our leadership team's behaviors serve as a positive role model for employees.               _____

10. We implement appropriate interventions to promote and/or address key behavioral issues within our organization.               _____

11. Our employees actively listen to our customers to understand their needs.               _____

12. Our employees demonstrate sensitivity/concern when servicing customer needs.               _____

13. Our employees demonstrate the behavioral savvy needed to deliver engaging, memorable experiences for customers.　　　　＿＿＿＿＿＿
14. Our employees go to extraordinary lengths to "Wow" our customers.　　　　＿＿＿＿＿＿
15. Our employees know when and how to "break the rules" to make a situation "right" for the customer.　　　　＿＿＿＿＿＿

**Based on the rating assigned, add each of the individual item ratings to arrive at a total score.**

Score of 45–60: Strength to capitalize on; you have the behavioral dimension characteristics of a LEADING PRACTICE brand.

Score of 30–44: With targeted and committed improvement, behavioral dimension characteristics could be elevated to LEADING PRACTICE brand.

Score of less than 30: Lots of opportunity for improvement; with diligent and careful effort, behavioral dimension characteristics could be elevated to LEADING PRACTICE. Start with low-hanging fruit!

We highly recommend that several key players in the company complete this assessment individually. Then compare the results. Where are the gaps in perception and practice? Why? Begin a targeted action plan to begin addressing the gaps and "low-hanging fruit."

# BRAND ELEVATION RESOURCES

Below are a few resources available at the time this book was published. We invite you to check out our Web site for more valuable brand-elevating programs and tools as we continue to expand our library of resources. Get more information on all of these products and more at: www. BrandAscension.com/Products_Resources.html.

## EBOOKS:
**THE 6 MYTHS OF SMALL BUSINESS BRANDING**: *Uncover the myths and learn the truths to exponentially elevate your business and bottom line!* With workbook (.pdf) + BONUS: Audio Narration CD, ++ BONUS: Brand Assessment Tool +++ BONUS. Additional Coaching Tips and Stories weekly via e-mail for seven weeks.

## GETTING YOUR EMPLOYEES ON THE BRAND WAGON:
*Learn the secrets of highly successful brands and how they engage the hearts and minds of their employees to deliver consistent and distinctive brand experiences.* With workbook (.pdf) + BONUS: Brand Assessment Tool ++ BONUS. Additional Coaching Tips and Stories weekly via e-mail for nine weeks.

## TOOLS:
**BRAND ASSESSMENT TOOLS** (Individual or six-pack).
Utilize these practical assessment tools to evaluate and assess where your small-business brand is now compared to best practices. Our brand assessment tools will help you reveal your brand's *"low-hanging fruit"* so you can begin implementing a *targeted* brand strategy that positively impacts your brand perception and behaviors!

## LIVING YOUR BRAND MANAGER'S ACTIVITY GUIDE
Now you can continue the enthusiasm for your brand and communicate your brand through a series of customized brand activities that reinforce your unique Brand DNA and keep your brand attributes top-of-mind with your employees. Through a step-by-step process you and your managers can facilitate these activities monthly to perpetuate team building, gain camaraderie, and help them live and embody the brand everyday!

## BRAND TRAINING:

**IGNITE YOUR BUSINESS BRAND DNA** (online course): Four-module course (each one hour of do-it-yourself, self-paced, online training) plus workbook to complete your unique Brand DNA. Follow a pre-recorded facilitation of this program at your own pace and with your employee team. Do the teamwork assignments and build your unique Brand DNA and begin implementation immediately.

## BRAND DNA GRADUATE TRAINING PROGRAMS:

**BRAND SPEAK: Learn How to Talk Your Brand Walk!** Continue your brand mastery by creating and applying unique vocabulary to your internal and external communications. Create unique ways of speaking about and marketing your brand through social media, Web sites, brochures, and internal communication pieces.

## 5 STEPS TO A ROCK SOLID ON-BRAND CULTURE:

Inspire and Motivate Your Employees to Deliver "On-brand" Every Time. A two-part online training video series designed for you and your employee teams to recreate your internal culture to be more brand inspiring and motivated.

**HOW TO MAKE YOUR BRAND MAKE $EN$E:** Create Brand-relevant Multi-sensory Experiences that Keep Your Customers Coming Back. A one-hour online training video designed to help you enhance your brand's customer experience through the senses.

## AFFILIATE MEMBERSHIP:

You can earn passive income by becoming a member of our BA Group Affiliate Member Program. It is free and gives you the opportunity to make money by referring the Brand Ascension Group products to your business colleagues and peers. Visit our Web site for more information.

# LIVING YOUR BRAND ACTIVITIES

The following activities will help you create a more consistent, "on-brand" environment for your business. They are designed to be engaging, interactive, and fun. Use these activities regularly with your employees to help them better understand that your brand is all about being authentic to what you stand for and consistently creating and reaffirming the desired perception in the minds of those who engage and associate with your brand (your customers).

## Activity #1: Observe and Celebrate Your Values and Style in Action

The purpose of this exercise is to have your employees observe your values and style in action within your internal environment. Successful branding starts internally with the passion and inspiration your employees have and demonstrate for your brand and how they emulate the brand at every opportunity. This is something your staff needs to observe and celebrate as a team to recognize, reinforce, and enhance the value proposition your brand has for them and for your customers.

List your values and style attributes on a flip chart or white board. Ask your employees to consider situations where they have observed these values and style attributes in action within your environment both internally (with employees) and externally (with customers). Discuss these occurrences and how they have reinforced and reaffirmed the brand in how it made people feel and the end result.

Let this discussion be ongoing. Keep coming back to it in your team meetings with your employees. Promote and celebrate examples of positive behaviors and situations through e-mail, personal interactions, team meetings, your internal and/or external newsletter, and your intranet. Post these examples of positive behaviors on the bulletin boards in your staff break room areas. Highlight these situations on a regular basis so they are top-of-mind sharing on how your employees are living and emulating the brand. Ask your employees to send acknowledgements and commend a colleague when they observe these attributes in action.

Ensure that you speak about your values and style at every opportunity. Weave this into your team meetings and reference examples as they occur. Celebrate with a pizza party or pot-luck lunch at every opportunity to acknowledge the positive behaviors occurring within your business. You'll be amazed at the results!

**Activity #2: Develop Your Unique Brand Speak (Vocabulary)**

Brand vocabulary is a distinctive and meaningful way to reflect your unique and distinctive brand attributes both internally (with employees) and externally (with customers). Why is it important to building a distinctive brand vocabulary? There are several reasons:

- Words provide an expressive means, a repertoire of communication that people can share with a common comprehension.
- Words are tools that cultures create and utilize to express themselves for the sole purpose of being understood.
- Specific vocabulary helps businesses define their brands through their culture, eliciting the desired emotions that create passion and inspiration.
- Words reinforce the essence of your brand—its uniqueness— in a language that is consistent, relevant, and distinctive.

Bring a group of your employees together and ask them to identify key internal (employee) and external (customer) touch points such as phone greeting, face-to-face greeting, responding to an employee request, customer issue or complaint, conducting a transaction with a customer, presenting a proposal or sales pitch to a customer, etc. As a group, develop a special brand vocabulary for your brand. Get creative and think outside the box!

1. List your values, style, and Brand Platform on a flip chart or whiteboard.
2. Brainstorm and agree on brand-relevant words that reflect each of your unique Brand DNA values, style, and your Brand Platform.
3. Share the following examples to activate your employees' creativity.

**Example #1:**

Ritz Carlton is known for their elegance, consistency, and outstanding treatment of their guests. They have paid close attention to their words and vocabulary within their brand delivery and experience a Brand Platform of "We are ladies and gentlemen serving ladies and gentlemen." They have what they call their Gold Standards of Service. These service principles and Brand Platform show up in how they behave and how they live and embody the essence of what they stand for. When you visit or stay at a Ritz Carlton, these Gold Standards and Brand Platform are reinforced in their language with elegance and sophistication, such as:

> a.   *Good Morning Ms. or Mr. vs. Hi or Hello*
> b.   *Most Certainly or It is My Pleasure, vs. OK; No problem*

**Example #2:**

A well-known media company has a Brand Platform of Entertain, Engage, and Excel. Their style is hip, confident, and creative. Their values are people, excellence, innovation, and community. See below how they weave specific verbiage into their interactions with customers at key touch points:

1.   Greeting a customer.

> *Ex: "****Hi****, welcome to _____, your **local partner** in media **innovation.** This is Shelly, how can I help?*

2.   Responding to a customer request, complaint, or issue.

> *Ex: "As **your** media **partner**, we are **passionate** about **your** success! Let's **get clear** on your needs ..."*

1.   Develop your specific vocabulary that reflects the essence of your brand.
2.   Start infusing your new vocabulary at every opportunity within your business. Observe how it changes the manner in which you deliver on your brand and reflects the essence of who you are.

## Activity #3: Create a Unique Brand Shake as a Ritual in Building Your Culture!

People learn culture and create rituals to express it. That, we propose, is one of culture's essential features. Culture is a set of learned behaviors and rituals common to a given group or society and serves as a template to cultivate behavior. It has predictable form and content, shaping behavior and consciousness within a group or society from generation to generation.

Culture resides in all learned behavior and in some shaping template or consciousness prior to behavior as well. If the process of learning is an essential characteristic of culture, then teaching it is a crucial characteristic. The way your culture is taught and reproduced is itself an important component of your distinctive culture.

Ask your employees to identify companies that have a unique culture both internally and externally. Harley-Davidson is a great example of a culture that has become a ritual. Their brand's promise is all about delivering complete freedom and comradeship of kindred spirits to avid cyclists. They have carefully leveraged their brand to create a community unlike any other in the world. They understand and capitalize on the power of their brand symbols on the plethora of products they produce and sell, such as leather clothing and accessories, screensavers, bandannas, iPod videos, etc.

Harley-Davidson supports and encourages HOG—Harley Owners Group—comprising hundreds of thousands members globally. They sponsor rallies, road tours, festivals, and celebrations that support freedom and comradeship for those that experience their brand. These keep their customers loyal and reinforce ongoing rituals.

What brands come to mind in representing powerful cultural rituals? Have your employees identify as many as they can think of. This will help them to understand the power of reinforcing and shaping your brand's culture through rituals.

Ask them what culture they represent. Take them through the following exercise to begin to create a simple ritual that reaffirms your brand.

## *Exercise*

1. Provide a copy of your Brand DNA to your employees, and particularly focus on your style and values and your Brand Platform and Promise.
2. Ask them to invent a distinctive Brand Shake (handshake) to introduce into your culture and that represents your brand.
3. Place employees into groups of three or four and create a contest for developing the official Brand Shake for your brand.
4. Select the most distinctive handshake that emulates your brand.
5. Name the Brand Shake.
6. Illustrate the Brand Shake on a flip chart to teach everyone in your business how to do it.
7. Have them practice the Brand Shake and demonstrate it at every opportunity. Business owners and management can take the lead in infusing the Brand Shake into your business.

For future considerations, have your employees brainstorm additional rituals you can introduce into your culture to reinforce and reaffirm your brand. These rituals will only strengthen your culture over time. Strong cultures are essential to building a powerful brand where employees are passionate and inspired.

# ENDNOTES

## PREFACE

1. U.S. Small Business Administration Office of Advocacy, September 2008.
2. The Economic Impact of Women-owned Businesses in the United States, 2009, Women's Business Research Center, http://www.womensbusinessresearchcenter.org/Data/research/economicimpactstud/econimpactreport-final.pdf.
3. U.S. Small Business Administration Office of Advocacy, September 2008 Survival and Longevity in the Business Employment Dynamics Database, Monthly Labor Review, May 2005. Redefining Business Success: Distinguishing Between Closure and Failure, Small Business Economics, August 2003.

## CHAPTER 1

1. Carlson Marketing International Study, 2001
2. James C. Collins and Jerry I. Porras, *Built To Last: Successful Habits of Visionary Companies* (New York: HarperCollins Publishers Inc., 2002).
3. Study conducted by the Aspen Institute and Booz Allen Hamilton: Chris Kelly, Paul Kocourek, Nancy McGaw, and Judith Samuelson, *Deriving Value from Corporate Values,* 2005 (http://www.aspeninstitute.org/publications/deriving-value-corporate-values).

# CHAPTER 2

1. Martin Lindstrom, *Brand Sense: Build Powerful Brands through Touch, Taste, Smell, Sight, and Sound* (New York, NY: Free Press, 2005).
2. Brand Scorecard concept adapted from Robert S. Kaplan and David P. Norton, *The Balanced Scorecard: Translating Strategy into Action* (Watertown, MA: Harvard Business School Press, 1996).
3. Howard Schultz and Dori Jones Yang, *Pour Your Heart into It: How Starbucks Built a Company One Cup at a Time* (New York: Hyperion, 1997), p.133.
4. Business Week, "Customer Service Champs," March 5, 2007.
5. Zappos.com, http://about.zappos.com/.

# CHAPTER 3

1. Brad VanAuken, *Brand Aid: An Easy Reference Guide to Solving Your Toughest Branding Problems and Strengthening Your Market Position* (New York: AMACOM, 2003), p. 38.
2. Duane E. Knapp, *The BrandMindset®, How Companies Like Starbucks, Whirlpool, and Hallmark Became Genuine Brands and Other Secrets of Brand Success* and *The BrandPromise®, How Ketel One, Costco, Make-A-Wish, Tourism Vancouver* (New York: McGraw-Hill, 2000)*and Other Leading Brands Make and Keep the Promise that Guarantees Success.* (New York: McGraw Hill, 2008), p. 75 in The BrandMindset®.
3. Watson Wyatt Worldwide, *Effective Communication: A Leading Indicator of Financial Performance-2005/2006 Communication ROI Study*™ (http://www.watsonwyatt.com/research/resrender. asp?id=w-868).

# CHAPTER 4

1. Howard Schultz and Dori Jones Yang, *Pour Your Heart into It: How Starbucks Built a Company One Cup at a Time* (New York: Hyperion, 1997).
2. Martin Lindstrom, *Brand Sense: Build Powerful Brands through Touch, Taste, Smell, Sight, and Sound* (New York: Free Press, 2005), p.83.
3. http://psychology.about.com/od/sensationandperception/a/color_green.htm
4. http://psychology.about.com/od/sensationandperception/a/color_blue.htm
5. Terry R. Bacon and David G. Pugh, *Winning Behavior: What the Smartest, Most Successful Companies Do Differently* (New York: AMACOM, 2003).

# CHAPTER 5

1. B. Joseph Pine II and James H. Gilmore, *The Experience Economy: Work Is Theatre & Every Business a Stage* (Watertown, MA: Harvard Business School Press, 1999).
2. Karen Leland and Keith Bailey, *Customer Service for Dummies®, 3rd Edition* (Indianapolis, Indiana: Wiley Publishing, Inc., 2006).
3. Duane E. Knapp, *The BrandMindset®, How Companies Like Starbucks, Whirlpool, and Hallmark Became Genuine Brands and Other Secrets of Brand Success* (New York: McGraw-Hill, 2000), p. 25.

# CHAPTER 6

1. Janelle Barlow and Paul Stewart, *Branded Customer Service: The New Competitive Edge* (Berrett-Koehler Publishers, Inc., 2004), p. 45.
2. Duane E. Knapp, *The BrandMindset®, How Companies Like Starbucks, Whirlpool, and Hallmark Became Genuine Brands*

*and Other Secrets of Brand Success* (New York: McGraw-Hill, 2000), p. 7.

# CHAPTER 7

1. Brad VanAuken, *Brand Aid: An Easy Reference Guide to Solving Your Toughest Branding Problems and Strengthening Your Market Position* (New York: AMACOM, 2003), p. 24.

# CHAPTER 8

1. Marc Gobé, "Why Advertisers Still Don't Get It," *Business Week,* February 16, 2007.
2. B. Joseph Pine II and James H. Gilmore, *The Experience Economy: Work Is Theatre & Every Business a Stage* (Watertown, MA: Harvard Business School Press, 1999), p. 12.

# CHAPTER 3 EXERCISE

1. Brad VanAuken, Brand Aid: An Easy Reference Guide to Solving Your Toughest Branding Problems and Strengthening Your Market Position (New York: AMACOM, 2003), p. 37.
2. Duane E. Knapp, *The BrandMindset®, How Companies Likes Starbucks, Whirlpool, and Hallmark Became Genuine Brands and Other Secrets of Brand Success* (New York: McGraw-Hill, 2000), p. 33.

# INDEX